GREAT WESTERN SAINTS AND SINNERS

By the same author

Great Western Steam
Great Central Steam
North Eastern Steam
North Western Steam

1. (*Frontispiece*) Hawksworth County No. 1013 (W91) leaving Chester.

Great Western
Saints and Sinners

W. A. TUPLIN
D.Sc., F.I.Mech.E.

London
GEORGE ALLEN & UNWIN
Boston   Sydney

First published in 1971
Second impression 1983

© George Allen & Unwin Ltd, 1971

ISBN 0 04 385057 X

Printed in Great Britain
in 11 point Plantin type
by Richard Clay (The Chaucer Press) Ltd,
Bungay, Suffolk

PREFACE

In view of the constant reshuffling of laudatory information about the Great Western Railway in books published in the last quarter-century, the reader may think that there is something very odd about mentioning 'sinners' at this stage. It is in fact merely the consequence of recording observations made without privilege and consequently without obligation. In this subject one did not need to go to the bottom of a well to find truth; it sufficed to go on to overbridges, on to station platforms, and into trains and to use one's eyes, ears and nose. One might also go into sheds and works where a steel tape-measure could find figures that would astonish compilers of lists of officially-quoted dimensions of Great Western locomotives.

The average Great Western enthusiast knew that there could be no such things as sinners anywhere on the Great Western system. There was no hint of such imperfection anywhere in the extensive literature on the subject. Its history was bland where it was not brilliant. No ripple sullied the effortless tenor of the Great Western way of life.

When the driver of a Paddington-Plymouth express told you at Newton Abbot that he had had to take it easy on the way because the fireman had had to go right back into the tender to bring more coal forward, and that he (the driver) was not going to do that sort of work and they ought to provide a third man, you thought he was joking.

When in later years you saw two young men from the shed get into the tender of the engine of a down express at Exeter and shovel coal forward, you thought it was very nice of them and what a pity they could not do it for the men on the Limited that went on to Plymouth without stopping at Exeter.

When you thought that they took a long time to put three coaches behind the up Limited at Exeter, you decided that it was because they were taking special care not to disturb the passengers in either part of the train.

When one realized that at the end of the Dean period one might have found in Great Western locomotive stock over 2,000 engines with no two identical, one simply thought 'How fascinating!'

When one was told how a passenger train got loose in the Severn Tunnel, one could see that so long as there were signals and smoke on the slopes it was bound to happen eventually, and, provided that someone remembered to break the warning wire it need not endanger passengers much although it could be puzzling to permanent-way men.

No matter what one saw on the Great Western, one could never believe that there was anything wrong about it because no printed word even remotely suggested such a thing. One almost reached the point of deciding to limit one's learning about the Great Western to what one could read and not to run the risk of getting a distorted picture by looking for oneself.

Now although, on the whole, the Great Western in the twentieth century did better than most other British railways (this could be seen by shareholders, and no one else really mattered) it did not achieve perfection in everything. It was to give a hint of this that the title of this book was extended to include the common antithesis to Saints.

In this book we shall neither quarrel with those who hold that the Great Western was the best British railway nor side with those who deem it faultless, but we admit that it was good enough to write about more than once.

ACKNOWLEDGEMENTS

The writer is indebted in some degree at least to almost everyone who has contributed to the vast literature of Great Western locomotives and also to the numberless writers of adjacent material that slowed down his researches with fascinating diversions.

As a source of information about historical details of Great Western locomotives, there is nothing comparable with the multi-volume work published by the Railway Correspondence and Travel Society with the title *The Locomotives of the Great Western Railway,* and the writer is happy to make very special acknowledgement of its value and to applaud the skill, care and industry of all those who contributed to its production.

In connection with a technical matter that interests many students of Great Western practice, the writer is glad to be able to reproduce a drawing by Mr E. J. Nutty of the notched double quadrant used with Great Western pole-type reversing gear. This drawing was published in 1948 in Mr Nutty's booklet about Great Western piston valves and valve gear.

Notes on the probable inspirations at Swindon for the names of the Ladies were completed with the assistance of members of the staff of the University of Sheffield and of the City Library of Sheffield.

Notes on the saints whose names were applied to Nos. 2911 to 2930 were derived from the *Penguin Dictionary of Saints* by Donald Attwater.

Much use has been made of the vast amount of information in the *Railway Magazine,* the *Locomotive Magazine* and the *Engineer.* For the job of extracting the numerous parts of it relevant to this book, the writer regrets to record that he is indebted to no one; he just had to do it himself.

Line drawings of broad-gauge locomotives have been derived from the magnificent series made by G. F. Bird and reproduced in the *Locomotive Magazine* in 1903.

ACKNOWLEDGEMENTS

ILLUSTRATIONS

Very valuable assistance in locating and providing photographs for reproduction in this book came from Mr Kenneth Leech, Mr R. W. Miller, Mr P. J. T. Reed, Mr R. F. Roberts, and Mr W. O. Skeat.

The writer is specially indebted to Mr F. Pascoe (who took the original photograph), to Mr Reed and to Mr Leech for the means of reproducing the picture of *Lady of Lyons* as built. That of *Saint David* was derived from a photograph by Mr Leech.

The photograph of 2/4-6-0 County No. 1013 reproduced as the frontispiece was taken by Mr J. R. Carter of Mayfair Studios.

Mr J. Spencer Gilks took the photograph reproduced on p. 160B.

BIBLIOGRAPHY

1. *The Locomotives of the Great Western Railway* (eleven parts), Railway Correspondence and Travel Society.
2. *An Outline of Great Western Locomotive Practice*, H. Holcroft, (Locomotive Publishing Co.).
3. The late G. J. Churchward's locomotive development on the Great Western Railway. K. J. Cook, O.B.E., in *J.Inst. Locomotive Engineers* No. 214, March 1950.

NOTATION

In this book, the usual Whyte convention is used to define the wheel-arrangement of any locomotive. The addition of T denotes side-tanks; PT pannier-tanks; and ST a saddle-tank.

Unless the locomotive has two inside cylinders and no others, the number of cylinders is added in front of a / preceding the Whyte designation. If the locomotive uses compound expansion, C precedes the /.

Pages 185 to 191 contain leading dimensions of some classes of Great Western engines built in the twentieth century and of typical classes of earlier engines. (A full list of the pre-1900 classes would be unwieldy.) For the reader's convenience, each item in these tables has a 'reference number', e.g. W44 for the Churchward Cities. This is quoted wherever the class is mentioned in the text so that the reader may quickly locate the basic facts about it.

CONTENTS

ﰤ

CONTENTS

ILLUSTRATIONS

ILLUSTRATIONS

ILLUSTRATIONS IN TEXT

ILLUSTRATIONS

CHAPTER I

Introduction

This is not a history of the Great Western Railway. Who could outsparkle McDermot? It is not even a factual history of Great Western locomotives; that is to be found for good and all in the multi-volume work published by the Railway Correspondence and Travel Society. This book is, however, about Great Western steam, and a fair question might be, 'Hasn't everything possible been written about that subject, time and time again?' The answer to that question is either 'No!' or 'Yes, but not so skilfully as to present a complete picture.' The triumph-song has gone on too long without a flaw and even the most fervent admirers of Great Western steam are beginning to get suspicious. An ex-Great-Western engineer was once chided for apparently believing that 'all Swindon's geese are swans'. We are far past that. Many people must by now have been persuaded that Swindon chicks are (or were) white doves of the Holy Grail. Others, however, have not been deceived and are inclined rather to resent the repeated fanfare. It looks like protesting too much. Every book has a 'blurb', but Great Western books tend themselves to be blurbs. How much – if anything – is there behind all the blah?

After having read, over the years, books on *Caerphilly Castle* and on *The King of Railway Locomotives* and on *The Castles and Kings of the Great Western* and on the *Kings and Castles of the GWR* and on *Western Region Castles and Kings* and so on, one might be excused for thinking that the only Great Western locomotives worth mentioning were the Castles and Kings. To get a less distorted picture of traction on the Great Western Railway after World War I it is useful to reflect that over the period

1923–1950, in which about 200 Castles and Kings were built, the Great Western placed in service over 2000 locomotives of other classes. On the eve of nationalization of British railways in 1948, the Great Western had about thirteen other locomotives for every Castle and King.

Of the less sung classes, the most distinguished were the Saints – their numbers by then depleted – and the other 2/4–6–0s built from similar components. For the purposes of a title all these may be classed as Saints but unsaintly Great Western features were not too rare to justify mention.

Of course there were no real sinners on the Great Western any more than there were any saints. But colourless though the Great Western may have been in these respects, it had some droll characters at times. When the elegant company of eighty Dean singles, heavily and fussily draped, gliding gracefully over the Great Western main lines, had been rudely fluttered by a group of Swindon-built American giantesses, stamping about in the nude except for their golden Great Western hats, what blithe spirit slapped the name 'Lady Superior' on the ringleader? It was very shocking and after nine more of the newcomers had been named as ladies someone complained to the management. As a result the next lot of outcoming ladies were fitted with mini-skirts and named as saints, hand-picked from the roster and applied in alphabetical order. The name of Saint Christopher was omitted; sight of it might have upset those travellers who had forgotten to take out insurance policies.

Now make no mistake! Whatever you might think about their looks, the Great Western Saints were grand goers. They set a fashion that spread to the LMS in thirty years and even to the LNER in another eight. When British Railways had studied the design of a general-purpose mainline locomotive, the best they could think of in 1950 was a Saint adapted to current needs and ideals. So the BR Standard Class 5 2/4–6–0 came out as a hatless, high-skirted Saint with free access to exposed essentials and a rattling ride for the men.

On the Great Western, however, Saints failed to win the star role as a trio of flashy French models were strutting round. They took the boss's eye and held it. They persuaded him to start a family that ran all the Great Western stat turns, but it may be doubted whether its extensive reproduction was altogether wise.

In what follows we look at some of the oddities in Great Western locomotive development and are led to wonder whether it ever produced anything better than the Saints. Whether there was in Great Western stock or staff anything to which the word 'sinner' might justly be applied is something that perusal of this book may help to elucidate.

The author confesses that his original interest in Great Western steam was not technical; at the age of three it could hardly have been so. When, many years later, he did start to examine the whys and wherefores on the basis of physics and mechanics, tempered with common sense, he found much to admire. But still the words 'Great Western' convey to him a moving picture wired for sound of a double-frame locomotive with flickering fly cranks and tittering pump valves speeding through lush countryside. The word 'American' means to him the downward and backward sweep of a connecting rod and coupling rod across the spoked circles of fully exposed coupled wheels.

His impression is that many enthusiasts share his admiration for Great Western double-framers, old-fashioned, out-of-date and expensive though they were. To us, Churchward's building of new locomotives of that description as late as 1909 is heart-warming in its suggestion that in this respect he was perhaps as dotty as we. It looks as if there were a deliciously benign streak in this great man whose work at Swindon was so outstanding as to become a subject for endless discourses to the enthralled enthusiast.

But be assured that one might read books about locomotives, admire pictures of locomotives, admire the locomotives themselves, from the station platform, from the lineside or from the trains speeding behind them, study their design and construction, read the histories of their designers and builders, and do all this assiduously for half a century without gaining any hint of what locomotives were really like. On the road, these sublimely designed and superbly constructed steam engines were just dirty devils to man and beast. They bumped, swayed and rolled as they fought the restraint of the track. Most of the time they ran in any direction but straight ahead. They quivered and vibrated under the impacts of their own connecting rods. They shook the enginemen in their boots; they banged their heads on the cab roof; they burned the drivers' legs and the firemen's bottoms (unless firemen pulled the fire-hole flap up after every shovel-stroke); they chilled the men with fierce draughts, splashed them with water and blinded them with coal dust. To greater or lesser extents all locomotives behaved in these uncouth ways, and don't imagine that Great Western engines were any better than any of the others.

A realistic book about steam locomotives would be printed on wavy disjointed lines, with words misspelt, missing or half-hidden by black smudges to keep the reader constantly aware of what he is reading about. This is hardly practicable but it would be one way of conveying how uncompanionable could be that great friend of man, the steam locomotive, and how different it was from the smooth, lush adoration in much of its literature.

CHIEFS OF GREAT WESTERN STEAM

Motive power on the Great Western, till its end with nationalization in 1948, was successively in charge of

> Daniel Gooch   from 1837
> Joseph Armstrong from 1864
> William Dean   from 1877
> G. J. Churchward from 1902
> C. B. Collett   from 1922
> F. W. Hawksworth from 1941.

From 1864 till his retirement in 1896, George Armstrong was in charge of the Wolverhampton Works.

None of these men worked for any length of time for any company but the Great Western, and so for 110 years Great Western steam was in the hands of Herrenvolk of a purity even beyond the aspirations of the late Herr Hitler. No important job went to anyone from outside. For every such job that became vacant, there was someone inside who could probably do it better than could anyone from outside. For whatever purpose Swindon might want men, it bred them under its own control.

Swindon took no men from outside and there is a suspicion

that, until Churchward's time, it took no ideas either. But Churchward certainly made no mistake of that kind. He used experience (as demonstrated by practice) on other railways to the full in developing his standard designs. These were so effective that his successors had little need for new ideas on design and certainly no very remarkable one appeared in metal. The main responsibility of the chief mechanical engineer of a railway was to achieve economy in manufacture, running and general maintenance of locomotives. For this reason he should ideally be an administrator, well acquainted with manufacturing processes and with the problems of co-ordinating them. New design was only an intermittent necessity and on the Great Western not a burdensome one after the Churchward 'constructional kit' had been established and proved.

Gooch had got the Great Western going with double-frame engines, Armstrong and Dean had continued in the same way, Churchward had standardized single frames and outside cylinders for main-line duties, and his successors needed nothing different. They were men with good manufacturing experience and Hawksworth had also had responsibility in the drawing office.

At all times the chief mechanical engineer's department was self-sufficient and self-reliant. It took notice of what was being done on other railways, but after Churchward had made the most of this, very little more of it even twenty years later was deemed to be worth copying. By and large that attitude was justified.

CHAPTER 2

The First Fifty Years

BRUNEL

Any examination of early history of the GWR inevitably leads to its basic designer, Brunel, whose mark persists even yet on its original main line in the wide spacing of the tracks. George Stephenson recommended that railways anywhere in Great Britain should be laid to a common gauge of the early lines in Northumberland and Durham, because there would surely come a need to connect them. Brunel on the other hand, thinking big and broad, decided that something wider would be valuable. He could have had no evidence for this, but his tendency was always to the grand rather than to the meagre. He may have thought that it was better for the original plans to be wrong on the broad side; it left room to substitute something narrower if that should be proved to be preferable.

Brunel may well have chosen seven feet as the gauge for the Great Western Railway by use of the 'fifty-per-cent rule': if you are going to alter anything, it's hardly worth doing so by anything less than 50 per cent. Applied to rail gauge it meant a move from the mysteriously chosen 4 ft 8½ in. to the round figure of 7 ft. Brunel probably thought that this coincidence was an arithmetical approval of his natural instinct to make his railway half as big again as the existing ones.

Everyone knows of Brunel's broad gauge of 7 ft, but it is hard to find any specific mention of the height of the broad gauge. For the standard gauge, the height was nominally 13 ft 6 in., but a number of British railways had bridges that restricted rolling stock to as little as 13 ft. Brunel's loading gauge was 15 ft high over a central width of 3 ft, tapering outwards to 11 ft 6 in. wide at all heights between about 12 ft and 5 ft, and was 10 ft 6 in. wide below 5 ft. Drawings show that some broad-gauge locomotives had chimneys as high as 14 ft 10 in.

Brunel went ahead on the 7 ft gauge with such enthusiasm as to persuade investors to contribute to his Great Western enterprise on that basis. He must have been convinced either that narrow-gauge lines would eventually be converted to the broad gauge or that the broad gauge could monopolize a goodly area in the south and west of England and that a change of gauge in running into that area or out of it need not be seriously disadvantageous. It did not turn out (although no one could have known during the crucial period) that the broad gauge had any general superiority over the standard gauge and so Brunel's estimates of the future went awry. But it did leave more room for big boilers and big bearings on crank axles and this made it easier for Brunel and Gooch between them to provide the early Great Western Railway with larger and more powerful locomotives than their contemporaries elsewhere. Quite early, those engines showed the higher speed that Brunel promised on the broad gauge.

Brunel's character may be called dynamic but his greatest engineering achievements were static. His bridges, viaducts and tunnels have survived the severest tests of time; their functions are essentially static. Where there was relative motion, Brunel's instincts led him less happily. For the former, rigidity may be tolerable; for the latter, a little elasticity is worth a lot and a little lubrication works wonders. Brunel's longitudinal sleepers resting on piles gave the rails a support that was unnecessarily and undesirably rigid. Coaches could be provided with soft springs, but not so locomotives and to them even the flexible rail-on-transverse-sleepers construction could convey through steel tyres a harsher vibration than is normally found in land-based machinery. Many miles of longitudinally-sleepered track laid down under Brunel's authority were eventually replaced by track with transverse sleepers. Such track simply rests on the ballast but it is superior in service to Brunel's more closely tied-down 'baulk road'.

In this connection it is of interest to read the following excerpt from a letter written by Brunel to a pupil in December 1854 on the subject of bridges.

'Consider all structures and all bodies, and all materials of foundations, to be made of very elastic india-rubber and proportion them so that they will stand and keep their shape; you will by those means diminish greatly the required thickness; *then add 50 per cent.*

'I have found that there is not a single substance we have to deal with, from cast iron to clay, which should not practically be treated strictly as a yielding elastic substance and that the amount of compression or tension, as the case may be, is by no means to be neglected in practice any more than in theory.'

An outstanding expression of Brunel's originality and confidence is the noticeably flat-arched bridge that carries the Great Western main line over the Thames at Maidenhead. By comparison with contemporary practice the bridge was graceful but looked weak, and no doubt directors were worried and critical about it. To ease the strain on those inclined to blood pressure Brunel added to the underside of the bridge some impressive timbers that could have strengthened it considerably had there been effective contact between them. In fact there was none, but as none of the worriers knew this they believed that the bridge had been made safer by the timberwork, which was accepted as a temporary measure. When at length someone started pestering for a permanent reinforcement, the bridge had given years of satisfactory service without (so it was then revealed) any assistance from the timber.

There is an odd similarity between this engineering incident and a constructional feature of the Churchward two-cylinder engines. In line with the slide-bar brackets was a transverse plate extending upwards to a circular arc matching the underside of the boiler and therefore looking like a support for it. But like Brunel's Maidenhead bridge timbering Churchward's transverse plate did not touch the boiler while the engine was in service. It did, however, provide a seat for the front half of the boiler when certain sorts of repair made it necessary or useful to remove the large castings that formed the smokebox saddle and the cylinders.

In the earliest days of the Great Western Brunel included in his specifications for locomotives a clause that had an obvious semblance of good sense behind it, but that was shown by later experience to be unnecessary and undesirably restrictive. By 1830 a good deal of experience had been gained in the operation of stationary steam engines in driving pumps and rotary machinery. Such engines, for the most part, ran slowly and so the crucial component of the engine – the soft packing that minimized leakage of steam between the piston and the wall of the cylinder – did not have to slide very fast on the iron surface, nor was that the case in the early steam locomotives that moved trains of coal wagons at a speed of a few miles an hour.

Brunel, however, foresaw trouble at this point in a fast-running locomotive and so he specified that in any locomotive built for the Great Western the piston speed had not to exceed 280 f.p.m. at a running speed of 30 m.p.h. This led some designers into freakish constructions in some of the earliest locomotives supplied to the Great Western and this circumstance gave to its motive power department a very bad start and to the young Daniel Gooch a job that would have defeated any less hardy spirit.

A much-quoted remark of Brunel's was one made in reply to a question about a dangerous exploit that by pure luck did not produce disaster. Before traffic on the new main line had put many trains on it, any sufficiently confident official of the company might mount any locomotive that happened to be in going order and drive it in either direction on either track at whatever speed he could get out of her, pretty much as any member of the public may use any public road or motorway today. Brunel had done this at 50 m.p.h. on one occasion and reached his destination just before a train left that point to run in the opposite direction over the track he had just used. He was asked what he would have done had he seen the train coming towards him while he was in mid-flight. He replied, 'In such a case I would have put on all the steam I could command with a view to driving off the opposite engine by the superior velocity of my own.'

This remark demonstrates some rather loose thinking that may perhaps be excused by the fact that elementary dynamics had not been so widely taught before 1850 as since. Brunel's remark was sound enough to the extent that the faster he ran at the approaching train the more strongly would the mean velocity of the mass tangled by impact be in his original direction of motion but the point is hardly more than academic. What really did mean something was that the faster he ran, the more destructive would be the impact for everyone concerned.

Not unnaturally, Brunel was opposed to the proposal that government officials should be appointed to investigate the causes of all railway accidents. Every railway manager would resent the implied suggestion (well-founded though it was) that not every railway company was doing all it might to minimize accidents on its system. Brunel's remark that the railway officials knew more about the subject than did any government body was not very clever, if only because it added weight to the implied criticism. Furthermore, whatever truth there might have been in what Brunel said would gradually be eroded away as the government officials concerned gained wider knowledge of what went wrong on all the British railways and not simply on one of them.

One is reluctant to refer to Brunel's connection with the 'atmospheric railway'. It was such a flop and – one can now see – inevitably so, that the sinking of a lot of other people's money in the venture was wicked. But was it so obviously wicked at the time?

By 1847 the speed and power of steam locomotives had been very emphatically displayed on the Great Western Railway and not merely in occasional dramatic dashes but also in daily performance. At least one daily train was booked to run from Paddington to Exeter, 193 miles, in 4 hours 25 minutes, at an overall average of 44 m.p.h. All over Britain the steam locomotive was doing its stuff and eighteen years had elapsed since the Rainhill contest had diverted discerning minds from any further thought about working railways by stationary engines and wire ropes. So why should Brunel have been attracted by a scheme that depended on stationary engines and an elongated 'pea-shooter'? Perhaps, having seen that the atmosphere principle did at least work somehow over short distances, he thought that in case it should turn out to succeed over long distances, he ought to be in on it. If there were indeed any chance of success, he ought to be investigating the subject in the most practical way by laying and running an atmospheric railway. Some people believe that a spirit of truly broad-minded enterprise will try anything once and that it is a disgrace not to be in the forefront of every development in one's main field of activity. Such people inevitably back a number of losers and that's what Brunel and the South Devon Railway did in fitting up twenty miles of level line with the atmospheric system in 1847.

Although the name 'pea-shooter' was applied in derision to this device, that name was slightly misleading. The pea in a pea-shooter is (or was?) propelled from behind by air pressure higher than that of the atmosphere. An 'atmospheric train' was pulled by a piston propelled from behind by atmospheric pressure and opposed by a lower pressure maintained by a suction pump driven by the next stationary engine ahead of the train. The pea was blown along; the piston was sucked along. This was simple in principle although culpably optimistic when applied to a railway.

The obvious difficulty was to couple the piston inside the tube to the train outside the tube. There was no evading the necessity to split the tube all along its length so that the lower end of an arm projecting downwards from the underside of the first vehicle of the train should be in the tube and connected to the piston. Except where there was such an arm, the split in the tube had to be covered with something that made a pretty air-tight joint. Even a slight imperfection extending over three miles between pumping stations would cause the pump to suck in a great deal of useless air per minute.

Closure of the slit was effected by a leather flap which, when well greased and new, worked reasonably well, but in time became gradually less effective, and indeed the leather went brittle and began to break away from its fastenings.

But in some places there was trouble of another kind before the leather had become brittle. Adjacent rats found that they liked the grease on the leather and might even eat some of the leather itself. The news travelled by rodent grapevine and soon the flap was fizzing for miles and the pumps were doing a lot of dead horse work. A century later, the chemical industry would have developed a profitable rat-repellent in a month or two and perhaps also a dis-tasteful long-life grease, but chemical technology was not so highly developed in the 1840s.

Only one track was provided with the atmospheric tube and so neither Brunel nor anyone else was compelled to solve the problem of designing 'atmospheric pipes' to take trains through junctions. Even in the 1840s people were so gratified with any mechanical means of propulsion from town A to town B that no one worried very much over the auxiliary operation of disposing of a train when it reached its destination. There was no special difficulty if the railway system were confined to a single line and a single train, but anything much more complex than that would demand points and crossings and it is hard to see how the atmospheric principle could have been applied in such circumstances. The problem never became urgent as the atmospheric principle failed to cope with conditions on the very simplest system.

After less than a year of service the 20-mile-long flap required renewal at a cost of about £25,000 and as no superior alternative kind of flap had been discerned, atmospheric propulsion was abandoned in South Devon.

It was reported that the atmospheric railway between Exeter and Newton Abbott, using a vacuum of 16 in. of mercury, had pulled a train of 100 tons at an average speed of 35 m.p.h. (on level track) and that a 28-ton train was sucked along at a maximum of 68 m.p.h.

Brunel seems to have found little encouragement in such feats. He gave some thought to a design for an expanding piston to cope with the change from the 15-in. diameter tube already laid to the 22-in. diameter tube that he had decided would be necessary west of Newton. On that section steep grades had been tolerated in laying out the line on the understanding that the atmospheric system would be much less hampered by gradients than were steam locomotives. In actual fact a century had to elapse before anything but a steam locomotive ever hauled a train between Newton and Plymouth, but the steep gradients imposed on the locomotives far more stringent train-load limitations than were necessary on the Great Western main lines east of Newton Abbott. So long as that station was used as an engine-changing point, the disparity between the gradients east and west of it could be neutralized by use of locomotives appropriate to the routes but when London to Plymouth non-stop came to be required, the engines concerned had to cope with a 1 in 36 gradient that was a nasty aftermath of the pea-shooter phase. Indirectly, Brunel's misjudgement on that subject persuaded Churchward more quickly to the six-coupled Saints than might otherwise have been the case.

GOOCH AND THE BROAD-GAUGE ENGINES

The task of laying the Great Western Railway with immense earth works, bridges, and all the other static features of civil engineering was undertaken by the dynamic I. K. Brunel, while the locomotives and rolling stock – the dynamic elements – were under the care of the less dynamic Daniel Gooch. He lacked the slightly eccentric brilliance of Brunel but he was stronger on solid worth and his appointment as Locomotive Superintendent of the Great Western in 1837 was just what that company needed.

At the age of nineteen Gooch was a locomotive designer at the Stephenson Works at Newcastle and he was not quite twenty-one when he left to become responsible for provision and maintenance of locomotives on the Great Western. It was an exacting test, because not every locomotive manufacturer at that time was so fully aware as were the Stephensons of what was needed in designing and building reliable locomotives. Many of those delivered to the Great Western Railway, in compliance with orders placed before Gooch came along, were unreliable, but it was he who had to cope with their defects and there were few other men who could have done it. Working against time to get crippled locomotives back into service was always a hard job, but it was worse than hard in those early days when reliable sources of supply of sound material by Gooch's standards were not numerous.

Additional locomotives were required quickly and Gooch had a bit of luck in the first year of his struggles. He turned to his previous employer to find whether he could supply engines fairly quickly. Gooch was delighted to learn that two newly completed locomotives were standing idle because their would-be purchaser could not pay for them. Gooch knew these engines and knew that they would be far better than anything else he had seen in the southland. Even the fact that they were built for a less wide gauge than 7 ft did not put him off very much. He persuaded Stephensons to replace the axles by longer ones and so it turned out that

29

financial difficulties in a foreign land enabled the first two reliable locomotives to be bought by the Great Western Railway much sooner than would otherwise have been possible.

The first of these engines, *North Star* (a name to be applied later to another epoch-marking Great Western locomotive), was indeed delivered to Maidenhead six months before the railway itself had been laid to that point. In the ordinary way it would have been sent by barge along the Grand Junction Canal to be unloaded at West Drayton, but the engine was too heavy for available canal barges and was therefore taken by a Thames barge to Maidenhead. It must have seemed dramatic, or at least theatrical, at the time, perhaps justifying a headline such as '*North Star* from Newcastle barges into Maidenhead'. The engine worked (in due course) the first train from London into Maidenhead.

North Star (W1) was reliable but heavy on coke, and so Brunel and Gooch did a bit of 'redraughting', that multiply-repeated operation that was still being performed on British Railways a hundred and twenty years later. First of all the blast pipe and chimney are set accurately on one common vertical line, then the height and diameter of the nozzle at the upper end of the blast pipe are varied, and then, if the chimney has an internal petticoat pipe, that is varied also although this is not necessary if the chimney is a long one. The procedure is that one keeps readjusting things till one finds the greatest diameter of blast nozzle at which boiler pressure can be maintained with normal fuel and firing. Maintenance of pressure can always be achieved by contracting the nozzle sufficiently, and so no one need be 'stuck' on the problem, but the bigger the nozzle the less the back pressure on the pistons. *North Star* as turned out by Stephensons had evidently been well below par, as Brunel and Gooch between them made changes that cut down coke consumption quite nicely.

The general constructional style of *North Star* was used in all broad-gauge singles and also in most of the standard-gauge Great Western engines built in the nineteenth century. The axleboxes were in frame plates outside the wheels and were thus more readily accessible than axleboxes between the wheels. The frame plates hid fair areas of the wheels from external view and this gave an air of solidity and strength to the general appearance of the locomotive. There is no essential functional advantage in this but it was a feature much admired by many amateur observers of locomotives at work. Perhaps equally numerous were the observers who did *not* like the look of outside frames, and both groups might well be satisfied as during the nineteenth century there were plenty of examples of both styles of construction to be seen on British railways.

It was the swaying effect of reciprocating parts on short-wheel-base successors to the *Rocket* that led the Stephensons to reduce the trouble by using inside cylinders. They accepted the cost and complication of the crank axle, and also accepted the consequent freedom to use outside axleboxes for all axles, and that is how the outside frame appeared on the 2–2–0 *Planet* of 1831.

It can be recognized now that it was perhaps not the best possible technical change (and indeed the Stephensons abandoned it in a very short time), but it did make it possible for twentieth-century enthusiasts to see outside-frame engines spinning along with flashing outside cranks. They were magnificent to see, but too expensive for twentieth-century railways; it is good to record that one at least of such engines is preserved in working order.

Outside frames characterized Great Western standard-gauge locomotives throughout the nineteenth century though most of the broad-gauge engines had inside frames and completely exposed wheels. For many years outside frames produced at Swindon were slotted in *North Star* style and the top edges were in many cases curved; later on the straighter and unslotted outside frame style of the Wolverhampton works was used. The *North Star* type of frame on a 2–2–2 could be overstressed by side pressure transmitted from the flanges of the leading wheels to axle boxes at the bottom of the horns and therefore well below the longitudinal part of the frame, but on the other hand the sideways bending of the horns and the twist of the frame provided valuable lateral flexibility. Contrary to what appearance might have suggested, the old Great Western outside frames were flexible. The long, apparently rigid wheelbase of the 8 ft singles was not at all rigid. Had it been so, there would have been trouble on sharp curves.

A notable feat by Gooch and a Great Western engine of his design was recorded on May 1, 1844. The engine (*Actaeon*) was one

31

of the Firefly (W2) class 2–2–2s built by Nasmyth Gaskell & Co., Manchester, in 1841. The feat was to run a six-coach train from London to Exeter between 7.30 a.m. and 12.30 p.m. and to return between 5.20 and 10 p.m.; each trip included a number of stops to take water. Gooch helped in preparing the engine and drove it for all the 387 miles. During the time at Exeter he was concerned with company business and sat down for only about an hour. Recorded history says nothing about firing the engine and so it may be presumed that the job was shared by two or more men.

The first locomotive to be built in its entirety at Swindon works was a Gooch development of the *North Star* type. This was *Great Western* (W4) designed and built in thirteen weeks in 1846 in itself a great achievement. And the engine could perform at a high standard: in June 1846 it took a train from Paddington to Exeter and back in a total running time of 419 minutes for 387 miles, an average of over 56 m.p.h. This was very remarkable indeed for the period and was good publicity for the Great Western and the broad gauge. On another occasion the engine pulled a 100-ton train to Swindon, 77·3 miles, in 78 minutes start to stop. On this form it could certainly have made the easier return journey in 75 minutes, and 77 years later a Great Western train was first scheduled to do that daily.

Great Western had a hay-stack firebox and no upward projection from the boiler barrel. Except for the large dome formed by the top of the outer firebox the boiler was domeless a characteristic of many boilers built for Great Western engines in the twentieth century.

Because of the weight of the cylinder casting a steam locomotive tends to be front-heavy and so if the leading axle is behind the smokebox it sometimes tends to be overloaded. This tendency was brought sharply to Gooch's attention by the breakage of the front axle of *Great Western*. Within a few weeks an extra axle was added, to make *Great Western* into a rigid-frame 4–2–2. Fifty years later Dean 2–2–2s were rebuilt as 4–2–2s but in this case with leading bogies.

(In writing of events such as these the phrase 'fifty years' glides effortlessly from the pencil, but it is interesting and impressive to pause for a moment to realize what a long time fifty years really is,

a. Pearson 4–2–4T (Bristol and Exeter Rly) No. 44 (W7)

. South Devon Rly 4–4–0ST *Sol* (GW No. 2125), built 1866.

. Gooch 'single' *Prometheus*, built 1888.

3a. *Dido* (W20) built 1851.

b. No. 355 (W59), built 1866. One of the few photographs of a locomotive with two storm sheets in position.

c. No. 1195 (W60), built 1876.

d. No. 2626 (W116) Aberdare class.

at least when compared with the average life expectation of a human being. Think of all the experiences one may have or hope to have over a period of fifty years and then think, for example, of Great Western locomotives scurrying about the country day and night for all that time, and of William Dean at the end of it being reminded by the derailment of a 2–2–2 in Box Tunnel in 1893 that 2–2–2s do tend to have a lot of weight on front axles and being convinced that perhaps they would be better as 4–2–2s. History repeats itself, but it is apt to take its time over it.)

The 4–2–2 form of *Great Western* with some modifications was adopted as the design of the *Iron Duke* (W6) class of 4–2–2s built in 1847. One very distinct improvement was the inclusion of Gooch valve-gear instead of the old 'gab-motion'.

Stephenson valve-gear, developed in the Stephenson works but not by either of the Stephensons, had been first used in 1842 and was soon to supersede all its predecessors in Great Britain. Wishing naturally not to copy this product of his old employers, Gooch devised an inverse form of it. He suspended the expansion link from another link hanging on a fixed pin and made changes of cut-off and changes of direction by readjustment of the height of the trailing end of the valve-rod which thus became a 'radius rod'. The concave side of the expansion link faced forward instead of backward as in the Stephenson gear.

To the extent that the 4–2–2 wheel arrangement was adopted as the result of service experience it may be regarded as a logical one and certainly it was the basis of several graceful designs of locomotive. Feasting one's eyes on a picture of a Dean single (or even better, on the magnificent model of *Majestic* to be seen at South Kensington) one may, however, form the impression that there is something rather odd or indeed not quite right about them. However beautiful one may judge the engine to be, the plain fact is that it has too many wheels that cannot help it to pull. Out of eight wheels, only two at the most can possibly put a pull on the train. One realizes that although such an engine may be good and fast where it does not have to pull very hard, if it should come up against any strong opposition it may wish it had a better grip on the rails. Greasy rails can prevent an engine from starting its train, even on the level, because the so-called driving wheels are not driving. A few grains of sand on the rails would work wonders but the crew of *Iron Duke* could get no such assistance unless one of them went down on to the permanent way and threw sand on by hand.

Eventually sand-boxes were fitted, but in parsimonious style as designers in general were very reluctant to believe that a main-line engine would ever have to pull when running tender first. So back-sanding was often omitted.

With proper sanding gear, single-driver locomotives could do a great deal of the nineteenth-century passenger-train haulage on the flatter routes of Great Britain but bad weather on appreciable gradients could get them into trouble. So sooner or later someone was bound to cast a censorious eye on that idle rear axle in a 4–4–2 and to examine what difficulties there might be in replacing the rear wheels with larger ones that could be made to share the driving effort by being coupled to the driving wheels.

It was not surprising that Gooch should have tried out this idea. He ordered from his old firm, Robert Stephenson, ten locomotives of a design which was substantially that of the current standard broad-gauge single minimally modified to make a 4–4–0.

The desirability of mounting coupling rods on pins pressed into the wheel bosses persuaded the designer to place the frame plates between the wheels rather than on the outside of them.

So arose the Waverley or Abbot class (W12) with wheels fully exposed but so skimpily spoked as not to conceal the fact that the frame plates were shaped in the same general style as those of the singles.

These engines, built in 1855, were perhaps the first 4–4–0 loco-motives in Britain, although 4–4–0T engines had been built at Swindon as early as 1849. These latter had leading bogies, whereas the Waverley class 4–4–0s had not; they were certainly the only British 4–4–0s with that distinction and there were no doubt occasions when someone fervently wished that they did not have it. But in general the lateral flexibility of the frame plates was enough to let the engines get round curves.

Engines shedded at Swindon had nasty gradients to contend with in working to Gloucester and even worse ones on the way back. Box Tunnel and Dauntsey Bank could also be tough on singles returning to Swindon from Bath. On this account the Waverleys were first stationed at Swindon shed, which was also a good place for engines of new design, because it was close to the works and the designers.

A drawing of the Waverley class engine *Lalla Rookh* shows very thin spokes and a coupling rod not much thicker; one wonders whether it lasted long in those dimensions. 'Throwing their rods' was a failing of Victorian locomotives and *Lalla Rookh* looks well set to do a bit of that. It would be no serious criticism if she did; funny things happened to coupling rods and as late as 1952 a discussion of them by the Institution of Locomotive Engineers certainly did not give the impression that everything was known about them. Nevertheless no locomotive engineer needed to hesitate before specifying coupling rods as the means of taking some drive from one pair of wheels to another. Coupling rods came very early in the history of the steam locomotive and no alternative device has ever approached them in respect of low initial cost, low maintenance cost or reliability.

The Waverley class well exemplified the practice in broad-gauge design of fitting a combined splasher and running board extending over the whole length of the frame and fitting the wheel rims rather closely. Another broad-gauge characteristic was the provision of a railing, not merely a hand rail, near the outer edge of the running board and far enough away from the boiler to enable a man to pass between the two. If one had to examine the main mechanism of a locomotive while it was running one would be in less danger on a broad-gauge locomotive with outside frame than on any other. But if one had to get from the footplate to the front of an inside-frame broad-gauge engine such as a Waverley at speed one would be in great difficulty, even if one used the safety valve casing as an anchorage for a rope to hold on to while climbing over the coupled wheel splashers. Moreover, on these engines as on the singles, access to the motion was obstructed by the inverted laminated springs that loaded the two leading axles.

Although the eye of the locomotive enthusiast was most strongly attracted by the locomotives that pulled the main-line passenger trains, much more important to the railway company were the goods engines which were, in the vast majority, o–6–os. Gooch's engines of this description were in general in the style of *North Star* except that the frame plates were inside, i.e. between the wheels. These were completely exposed except for the fact that a shallow valance under the running board hid the tyre of each wheel where the running board was arched to clear it. (The only o–6–o exception to this was the Hercules class of four engines built in 1842.) Not until Bulleid produced the first Southern Class Q1 in 1941 did any o–6–o in Britain show more of its wheels than did the Gooch o–6–os.

On the Bulleid engines the boiler casing was wider than the rail gauge so that it might be expected to catch a lot of the splash thrown up by the wheels in wet weather. Bulleid therefore provided no splashers. Gooch probably regarded a running board of some kind as essential and thought it unreasonable to spray the men with water from below as well as from above. So he gave all his engines what were just about the skimpiest effective splashers.

Perhaps the most remarkable of the Gooch engines were the fifteen members of the *Corsair/Sappho* class (W10 and 11). These were 4–4–o saddle-tank engines, which is notable enough, but their structure was what later became that of the conventional steam roller, i.e. the boiler was part of the frame. The plate frame proper extended no further forward than the rims of the leading coupled wheels. The four carrying axles had axle boxes loaded by inverted laminated springs in a bogie that guided the engine laterally by force transmitted to the boiler through a ball-and-socket joint. One may be at first horrified to think of the boiler acting as part of the frame of a locomotive, but in fact the boiler shell is incomparably the strongest structural member in any ordinary steam locomotive and so stresses imposed on it by frame loading and piston loading would hardly be perceptible by comparison with the normal ones set up by steam pressure.

Nevertheless the steam-roller type of chassis was never much used in steam locomotives. Boilers periodically needed to be removed for major repairs and it was nice to be able to do this without leaving the rest of the locomotive in pieces. (But over fifty years after *Corsair* was first assembled, Churchward adopted at Swindon as standard a construction that permitted a locomotive to be divided in the manner suggested by the general layout of *Corsair*.)

A very interesting feature of *Corsair* was that the leading coupled wheels were flangeless; the engine was kept on the track by the flanges on the bogie wheels and rear wheels.

Side movement of the bogie relative to the frame was limited to what was permitted by flexibility of the loaded members. There was no spring or inclined suspension link to permit controlled side movement. This lateral location at the ends of the engine minimized the tendency to sway.

The scheme was extensively used in foreign countries, especially where severe curves almost demanded it. British practice was, broadly, to have flanges on all wheels and to give the bogie so much lateral freedom that it provided little lateral guidance; the flanges of the leading coupled wheels did most of the guiding of the locomotive into curves. This was basically dangerous, but we got away with it. They were not so lucky in other places; the Bihta derailment in India in 1937 was a consequence of this. The accident was investigated by a group of British engineers and after the contents of their report had been published it was decided that quite a large number of British locomotives would be safer with stronger side control of bogies. *Corsair* had been designed on much safer principles.

Another feature in which *Corsair* differed from conventional locomotive practice was in the use of sledge brakes pressed down on to the rails between the coupled wheels. There was no parallel to this in steam road rollers, but there was in electric tramcars many years later.

The saddle tank on *Corsair* was very deep at the front; it cuddled the boiler like a tea cosy. On the top of the tank was the semblance of a tea caddy to hold sand to be run from it by two pipes, each as nearly vertical as possible, down to the rails just in front of the driving wheels. G. F. Bird's drawing of *Corsair* shows no rod by which any sand valve could be opened by anyone on the footplate but it would be unfair to assume from this that no convenience of that type was provided.

Later engines of the *Corsair* design had sandboxes just above the rear bogie wheels and instead of the sledge brakes a brake applied

37

to the right-hand trailing coupled wheel. It was no doubt judged that the axles and coupling rods between them would spread the braking effort over the four lines of contact of coupled-wheel tyres with the rails.

The coal bunker extended for some distance behind the rear coupled wheels. The top edge of each side sheet was in the form of a half sine curve merging with the rear splasher and this was another resemblance to steam-roller practice. Access to the foot-plate from rail level on the right-hand side was gained by using two steps suspended from the rear buffer beam to reach the back part of the running board and then a high stride over the hand rail would land one in the coal that must have covered the foot-plate when a good supply had just been taken on. On the left-hand side, wheel spokes and coupling rod provided useful footholds for climbing on to the engine.

One would need a lenient and persistent eye to discover anything like beauty in an engine of the *Corsair* design. One would need to go from Devon to the diagonally opposite corner of England to find comparable ramshacklery in the looks of a local locomotive. But after all, that was where Gooch had come from!

Perhaps Gooch's unhappiest-looking locomotives were the twenty-two condensing-tank engines (W15) built in 1862–64 for running Great Western trains through tunnels of the Metropolitan Railway, which was laid with rails at both broad and standard gauge. Well tanks could be carried where the mechanism of an inside-cylinder engine would be and so Gooch led himself to the use of outside cylinders. A running board extended across the coupled wheels and the greater part of each cylinder was above it. The slide bars, markedly inclined to the direction of the rails, were almost completely hidden by the valance under the running board.

These engines resembled Sturrock's 2/0–8–0Ts for the same class of Great Northern service in that there was no specific accommodation for coal. It was dumped on the footplate and the driver built a pedestal for himself from a careful selection of stable-looking lumps.

Gooch consistently used raised fireboxes, domeless boilers, inside cylinders and 'sandwich' frame plates in his regular designs.

(The sandwich frame plate is a slab of wood sandwiched between two thin wrought iron flitch plates.) That the big-wheeled engines could really go is not surprising when one considers their high power-weight ratio. This is suggested by the high ratio of grate area (sq. ft) to total weight (ton). The former was large because the broad gauge left plenty of width for the firebox and the early engines at least were light for their size. This was partly because the low boiler pressure (about 60 p.s.i.) enabled the boiler to be made from thin plates and thin-walled tubes and partly because wheels were still in the spidery stage.

North Star's grate area of 13·6 sq. ft on a total engine-weight of less than twenty tons gives a ratio of about 0·7 whereas in latter day main-line engines the ratio was about 0·4.

Even in *Iron Duke* (1847) the ratio had come down to 0·6, partly as the result of strengthening the boiler to work at 115 p.s.i. In the last seven 8 ft singles to be built, the weight had gone up to nearly forty tons and the grate/weight ratio was down to 0·55.

To set against this decline, the raising of boiler pressure from 50 p.s.i. to about 120 p.s.i. certainly offered the possibility of getting more power per square foot of grate and some amateur students of locomotive practice have the impression (opposed to all the evidence) that this could go on for as far as one cared to raise the boiler pressure. This is, however, a naïve hope for which neither basic physics nor a century of practice provides any justification. If there had been anything in it, we should have had steam locomotives working at 300 p.s.i. and averaging 150 m.p.h. on the level.

No history, however detailed, of Gooch locomotives need include much on the subject of cabs, as Gooch never provided one. Perhaps his experience of engine-driving had been in uniformly clement weather. What good is a cab on an engine pottering along from Exeter to Newton Abbot on a warm summer day? Why have a cab on an engine that runs most of its distance in the Metropolitan Railway tunnels? Gooch may have asked such rhetorical questions but whatever answers there may have been they produced no cab. The main-line engines had weatherboards with circular windows, and although this was much better than nothing in cold weather the authorities made no attempt to provide the men with any protection against rain. The probability is that in wet weather the men huddled together within the outline of the boiler and relied on the back view of distant signals for suggestions that it was about time they took a bit more interest in where they were going.

But there was one man on the tender who was given some protection. This was the travelling porter who was supposed to keep watch over the train (at least in daylight) and to look out for any flag of distress displayed by the guard. If anything unusual suggested that a message should be conveyed to the enginemen, the travelling porter conveyed it. Normally he sat in a closely fitting hut (commonly called the 'iron coffin') mounted on the rear of the tender and facing backwards. On few days in the year would he find it too warm but at least he was not normally assailed by mile-a-minute raindrops. A safety belt in the form of a loop of rope could be worn by any travelling porter who feared that falling asleep might mean falling off. But danger from exposure in winter was considerable as the man in the iron coffin had nothing comparable with the hot boiler that the enginemen had in front of them.

So there were some infelicities in the working of trains on the Great Western broad gauge, as indeed there were in most industrial activities at that time, but by and large Great Western motive power was as good as any in Britain and better than some. It had not only met all demands but had blazed some dramatic trails.

By hard work Gooch won a battle against a desperate initial situation in the locomotive department of the Great Western Railway when he joined it. He then developed design, construction and operation of locomotives on sound lines and in 1864 he handed over the control of a good locomotive stock to his successor Joseph Armstrong, who came to Swindon works from the Wolverhampton works of the Northern Division of the Great Western Railway.

At that time (1864) the Great Western was still only a small railway with about 360 locomotives, of which about 160 were 0-6-0s and 120 were 2-2-2s. They worked from nine main running sheds and on an average week day there were fewer than 200 engines in steam. So there were usually as many engines idle as were working or ready to work; of the idle ones, about half would be under repair either at the works or at sheds. This was normal in the nineteenth century.

An unusual feature was that the broad-gauge engines bore no running number; they were identified solely by name. This singularity ceased in 1866 when the Great Western amalgamated with the Vale of Neath Railway and acquired nineteen unnamed engines. In 1876 there were amalgamations with the Bristol and Exeter Railway and the South Devon Railway, ninety-five locomotives from the former and eighty-five from the latter being thus added to Great Western rolling stock while over 280 miles of broad-gauge track were added to its static stock.

The largest number of broad-gauge engines existing at any one time was 419. The last one was built in 1866; it was the last of the six 0–6–0 side-tank engines (W23) of the Sir Watkin class.

PEARSON TANKS (W7) (BROAD GAUGE)

Among the most astonishing locomotives ever to run in regular service on a British railway were the eight 4–2–4 well-tank engines of the Bristol and Exeter Railway. They were built by Rothwell at Bolton in the period from 1853 to 1854 to the design of James Pearson, the Locomotive Superintendent of the B&E. Among their distinctions was a driving-wheel diameter of 9 ft – the largest ever used in Britain – and the multiple tying of the boiler to the frame. Ahead of the driving wheels were two transverse plates, about two feet apart, the rear one reaching up above the centre-line of the boiler, the other not so high and apparently bolted to flanges attached to the barrel. (One must say 'apparently' as the very similar plates on Churchward engines were not attached to the barrel.) The front end of the barrel was joined to a narrow wrapper-type smokebox, bulged at the bottom over the cylinders which were prominent above the running board.

In addition, the boiler had transverse brackets extended over the driving wheels and so received support from the four driving axleboxes through vertical rods and assemblies of four rubber rings enclosed in metal cylinders. The only brake blocks were between the wheels of the rear bogie.

One of these engines is said to have come down Wellington bank at over 80 m.p.h., which is not difficult there, and indeed application of the skimpy brakes would not have made much difference.

More significant information would be about the weight of train that any engine of this class could reliably take *up* Wellington bank without assistance.

These engines were scrapped in 1868–73 and four rather similar ones were afterwards built at Bristol. These had 8 ft 10 in. driving wheels, 18 in. × 24 in. cylinders, different wheel-spacings and fewer unconventional features. At least one (No. 40) had a cab in the form of a single sheet bent to form a front weatherboard, an all-over roof and a rear weatherboard.

The four engines came into Great Western stock with the take-over of January 1, 1876, and were numbered 2001 to 2004. As Armstrong believed cabs to be dangerous, each engine ran under Great Western rule with a front weatherboard but no rear one. No. 40 (2002) at least was given brakes on the wheels of the leading bogie and also acquired in the front and rear of each driving wheel a long narrow sand box extending from the running board down nearly to rail level.

By July 1876 No. 2001 had been repaired at Swindon and shortly afterwards, on July 27, ran off the road and overturned at Long Ashton on the approach to Bristol when working the up Dutchman, killing the enginemen. The driver, long used to the engine, had complained that she had not been running properly after returning from Swindon and that 'she would have him up in the hedge or down in the ditch'. This was consistent with tight fitting of the driving axleboxes in the hornblocks which were very much bigger than any previously seen at Swindon, where it was (even in 1876) the practice to leave less clearance in this crucial region than was given in B.&E. workshop practice.

(In 1951 an LMS Pacific left the road at Weedon as the result of tight fitting of bogie axleboxes. This arose out of an arithmetical error in conjunction with a bogie frame skimpy enough to allow an excessively wide axlebox to be inserted between the hornblocks without opposing suspiciously high frictional resistance and to allow attachment of the hornstays to clamp the axlebox.)

The four 4–2–4Ts were withdrawn from service after the Long Ashton derailment and No. 2001 was scrapped. The other three engines, Nos. 2002, 3 and 4, were rebuilt as 4–2–2 tender engines with 8ft driving wheels in 1876 and to create a bit of harmless confusion No. 2004 was renumbered 2001. These engines were finally withdrawn from service in 1890, 1884 and 1889 respectively.

ARMSTRONGS AND DEAN

Railways were booming in Britain when Daniel Gooch retired in 1864, but Brunel's broad gauge was on the way out. Disappointment about this may well have been a factor in persuading him to leave the railway to help in an aftermath of another Brunel adventure, the laying of the first trans-Atlantic cable by his giant ship *Great Eastern*.

Joseph Armstrong went from Wolverhampton to become Locomotive, Carriage and Wagon Superintendent at Swindon, whilst his brother George had a similar position at Wolverhampton, the headquarters of the northern division. Joseph died in 1877 and George retired in 1896.

Formerly Swindon and Wolverhampton works represented broad and standard gauge and operated independently of each other. With gradual abandonment of the broad gauge Swindon would become standard instead of broad, whatever superficial justification there might have been for separate works would disappear, and one would become a subsidiary of the other. This did indeed happen, but over thirty years had to elapse before it could be seen to have been accomplished and what was done at the two works during that time delighted the hearts of locomotive enthusiasts. There had previously been some semblance of standardization in locomotive stock built up by Gooch, but this was not at all obviously the case at Wolverhampton, partly because many of the locomotives had come from small railways taken over by the Great Western.

The Armstrongs had grown up surrounded by locomotives of varied origins and although they must have realized that real economy demanded standardization they were content to drift towards that ideal rather than to fight their way to achieve it quickly. They showed great reluctance to scrap any locomotive; they always preferred to modify or to rebuild a locomotive where improvement was required, rather than to scrap it and restart from scratch. William Dean, who succeeded Joseph Armstrong at

Swindon, pursued the same policy and between them they had provided for the Great Western Railway at the end of the nineteenth century as varied a collection of locomotives as could be found on any British railway except perhaps the North Eastern.

Engines had inside frames or outside frames or double frames and the frame plates themselves might be plates or sandwiches. Boilers might be domeless or might have domes in different positions on the boiler barrel. Outside fireboxes might be raised or not. Wheels of broad-gauge engines were (in general) fully exposed whilst those of standard-gauge engines with outside frames were fairly well hidden.

Dean engines carried structures that might be described, in a generous moment, as cabs but nothing on the Armstrong engines would suggest such a word to describe them. The Armstrongs themselves had been brought up on cabless locomotives to endure, or even to enjoy, the misery of wind and rain and said specifically that they would not deny Great Western enginemen the privilege of similar ennobling experience by providing them with cabs to hide under. What about (they asked, disdaining any hint about blowers) the chemical danger of breathing sulphurous gases that might come out of the fire hole and be trapped in a stuffy cab? They couldn't bear to think about it, they said, but neither George nor Dean raised any objection to the use of the Severn Tunnel (opened 1886) on the ground that the atmosphere might at times become a shade sulphurous.

Frame plates might be in the old Stephenson cut-away style or might be of more nearly uniform depth. The top edge of a frame plate might be straight or might have a wave over each axlebox. In a double-frame engine the crank axle might have axleboxes in the outside frames, or it might not.

When steel plates over 5 ft wide became available, Dean started to make certain boiler barrels from two rings instead of three, and then the dome might be mounted on either half of the length of the barrel.

The top of the bunker on a tank engine might have had any one of a score of different shapes. It is not certain that every engine had the same shape on both sides.

Saddle tanks sometimes extended over the smokebox and sometimes they did not; sometimes they extended right back to the cab-front and sometimes they did not. Saddle tanks were common on 0–6–0 tank engines, but side tanks were preferred on 2–4–0Ts or 0–4–2Ts.

Safety-valve casings and chimney tops showed varieties of forms. Water might be fed into the boiler at any two of a variety of points on it. In some barely credible cases the feed was into the side of the firebox.

A feature that was very nearly, if not entirely standard was a regulator-lubricator mounted on the smokebox immediately behind the chimney or on the saddle tank if the engine had one that extended so far forward. The case of No. 60, a double-frame 0–6–0ST, was exceptional in that it had at one time a regulator lubricator ahead of the chimney. It also had steam-condensing pipes, evidently because it was intended to be able to work in the tunnels of the Metropolitan Railway; as the only rain in a tunnel would be drips from the roof the engine had neither cab nor much more than a suspicion of a weatherboard.

During the period 1864–1879, standard-gauge locomotives put into Great Western service included the following:

Wheel arrangement	Number of engines	Number of classes	Average number per class
0–6–0ST	583	6	97
0–6–0	302	4	75
0–4–2T	176	1	176
2–4–0T	152	2	76
2–4–0	78	4	20
2–2–2	51	2	26

This brief table suggests very strongly that even on such a widespread railway as the Great Western, short distance movements represented the bulk of the traffic. An emphatic majority of the locomotive stock were 0–6–0s (this was so throughout Great Britain) and in this group there were nearly twice as many tank engines as tender engines. In this latter feature the Great Western was unique in Great Britain.

The average number of engines (apart from 0–4–2Ts) per class was not large and in most classes there were plenty of variations in detail and even in boilers.

Of the locomotives mentioned above Swindon built the tender engines and 140 of the 2–4–0Ts (571 altogether) and Wolverhampton built the remaining 771 tank engines.

During the Dean period the need for new classes of locomotives to be more powerful than their predecessors suggested the need for cylinders of greater diameter. The conventional arrangements, in which flat valves bear on vertical faces between the cylinders, limited the cylinder diameter to about 18 in. in a locomotive with an inside frame on the standard gauge. If the diameter were greater than this then the valves might be placed above the cylinders.

Where, as in a 2–2–2 or a 2–4–0, the cylinders were ahead of the leading axle and the centre lines of the cylinders were well above the axle, the valves might alternatively be placed below the cylinders. This arrangement had the advantage that the lid of the valve-chest could easily be removed. Then, if you didn't mind lying on your back, after withdrawal of the valve through the front opening of the steam chest you could see the port face and have direct access to it. (It would have been even better if you could have turned the locomotive upside down.)

This arrangement of valves was used in the thirty Dean 2–2–2 singles. Eight of them were built as broad-gauge convertibles and ran for some time on the broad gauge. The cylinders were large and their weight, overhanging the leading axle, may have been allowed by the designer to load it more heavily than was prudent. It may also have contributed to a bad 'nosing' action at speed. One of these engines was derailed in Box Tunnel in circumstances that suggested excessive weight on the leading axle and the whole class naturally came under suspicion. Dean saw, as Gooch had seen in similar circumstances in 1846, that the engines needed an extra carrying axle in front. Unlike Gooch, Dean decided that a leading bogie was required and, moreover, a bogie specially designed so that it could be withdrawn from under the engine without too much trouble as this would have to be done whenever the valves were to be examined.

The need for a bogie with this unusual facility upset no one at

Swindon as just such a bogie had been provided under a rather special 4–4–0 tank engine No. 1 (p. 61) built in 1880. It is true that the design used in that engine was not successful, but at least it gave Swindon some pointers on what not to do. The arrangement employed in the 4–2–2s was admirable in that it required only the removal of four locknuts and nuts to allow the front end of the engine to be lifted clear of the bogie. But there was room for variety in detail, and plenty of variety was to be found in the bogies of the 4–2–2s without considering any other components of the locomotive. Whatever one examined on a Dean single there was little to offend the eye of anyone who liked the looks of outside-frame engines.

The thirty 2–2–2s were all converted to 4–2–2s before the end of 1894. Fifty new engines of the 4–2–2 type developed in this way were built in the following five years.

On May 4, 1904, No. 3065 *Duke of Connaught* brought a 120-ton Ocean Mails train from Bristol (Pylle Hill) to Paddington in 99 minutes 46 seconds at a start-to-stop average of 71·3 m.p.h. and this regained for the Great Western the distinction of being a very fast line and indeed the fastest in Britain. Not for thirty years was any such sustained speed achieved in this country on any railway but the Great Western.

Endless variety was no fault in the eyes of any interested observer of Great Western locomotives. It conflicted, of course, with the principle of interchangeability of components between nominally identical locomotives, and so it was a luxury that not every railway could afford. The Premier Line – the London and North Western – had not been able to afford it for thirty years or more. On that line numerically large classes of identical locomotives had been the rule since Ramsbottom took charge at Crewe, and the difference in this respect between the 'North Western' and the 'Great Western' was aptly epitomized in the difference between the black painting of the locomotives of the one, and the polished brass and gay paint of the other.

Nor had the North Western ever been able to afford the luxury of a double-frame engine. The old Allen 'Crewe goods' 2–4–0 showed a tendency in that direction but Ramsbottom had limited himself to plain single frames and no successor on the North Western

47

could contemplate anything more costly. This came also to be the case on other railways, and the Great Western was the one to make the last stand in this field. It was not that Dean had failed to recognize that inside frames could meet all ordinary needs – his 260 class 2301 0-6-0s (W62) introduced in 1883 makes that point clear – but the double-frame tradition persisted ('Praise be!' say Great Western enthusiasts) and Churchward built double frame 4-4-0s as late as 1909. There in the last batch of Bulldogs the full panoply of Great Western double-framing was to be seen in one of the perkiest-looking lot of locomotives ever built. They were bright Birds indeed, and for 5 ft 8 in. wheelers they could fly too!

Going right back to the time of Gooch's superintendency one finds that in 1857-1861 Beyer-Peacock supplied to the Great Western six inside-frame 0-6-0s which, largely because of the shape of the coupling-rod splashers, looked like the North Western DX 0-6-0s, and this resemblance remained even after reboiling. This early trial of the elemental inside frame evidently failed to convince either Gooch or Armstrong that it had any appreciable advantage over the double frame. Dean seems to have been converted to the idea in 1883 as he then started to build the class 2301 single-frame 0-6-0s and went on doing so till 1899.

Even so, he built in 1885-1886 twenty class 2361 double-frame 0-6-0s, which fitted into a miniature standardization scheme started in 1884. Three classes were concerned in this scheme:

2-4-0	class 3201 Stella	25 engines (W30)
0-6-0	class 2361	20 engines (W63)
0-6-0ST	class 1661	40 engines (W71)

Cylinders, motion and springs were common to all three and the six-coupled engines had common frames. The boilers were generally similar but not identical.

The 2-4-0s soon went out of the standardization picture in respect of boilers. As the years went by there appeared many combinations of domed or domeless boilers, flush or raised round-topped fireboxes, flush or raised Belpaire fireboxes, long or short smokeboxes, long or short chimneys and so on.

An interesting example was the 3201 class 2-4-0 (W30) which

4a. No. 1 2–4–0T conversion from 4–4–0T (p. 51).

b. No. 1406 (W51). Note volute springs.

c. No. 4807 (W57).

5a. No. 322 double-frame 0–6–0ST (W67).

b. No. 3532 double-frame 0–4–2T (W53)

c. No. 3601 (W55). Smokebox overhangs buffer beam.

d. No. 3913 (W119) Churchward conversion from Dean 0–6–0 (W62).

started off on a vagrant foot, for the very first engine was sold in 1885 to the Pembroke and Tenby Railway (where it was numbered 8 and named *Stella*) before being used on the Great Western. When the smaller line was absorbed the engine became part of Great Western stock, was numbered 3201 and retained the nameplates that had been attached to its cab sides.

Stella class engine No. 3514 was fitted with the No. 3 boiler with raised Belpaire firebox well tapered in plan view. A noticeable feature was that the run of the reversing rod was hidden by the firebox lagging plate for a distance of a couple of feet abreast of the front half of the box. (See also No. 3558 p. 64A.)

The variety of reboilerings of the Stella class was a typical feature of most of the pre-Churchward locomotives on the Great Western: their ever-changing aspect was one of the great delights of the stock for the locomotive enthusiast. It seems unlikely that it could be equally delightful in the economic sense, unless indeed it was an expression of a make-do-and-mend policy that insisted on getting the last bit of useful life out of every engine by patching up with whatever could be found for the purpose in immediately available stock.

Right through the Armstrong periods (at Swindon and at Wolverhampton) Great Western main-line trains were run by six-wheel engines, apart from Gooch's 4–2–2s which were still used on the broad gauge. Weights of trains had been increasing over that period and so had weights of engines, so much so indeed as to approach the desirable limit for three axles. After the frolic of No. 3021 in Box Tunnel it was decided that all future Great Western 'flyers' were to have at least eight wheels.

This policy was implemented by starting in 1894 the 3031 class 4–2–2s widely acclaimed as the most beautiful of all locomotives, and by converting to the 4–4–0 arrangement four 2–4–0s that Dean was wondering what to do with. These rebuilds, with 7 ft. 1½ in. wheels, were in the same style as the 4–2–2s and perhaps surpassed them in beauty. Numbered 7, 8, 14 and 16 and named *Armstrong, Gooch, Brunel* and *Charles Saunders* they were commonly known as the Armstrongs (W34) and they were the only Great Western 4–4–0s in the purely Dean style.

The Armstrongs were undistinguished in service and when the

original 20-in. cylinders (which someone thought were too big) were replaced, after nearly ten years, by standard 19-in. cylinders, the Armstrongs remained undistinguished in service; not even tapered boilers and superheaters made any difference in this respect. They were rather nice-looking engines and not every class merited such acclaim.

It happened that the summer of 1894 was long and hot and that in consequence the damage of fires started in Devonshire by sparks from Great Western engines had been more extensive than usual. So attention was naturally directed to the provision of spark-arresting devices in the experimental designs.

Any spark arrester tends to weaken the draught on the fire, but least objectionable in this respect are smokebox baffles which compel the flue gases to move ahead of the blast pipe and then to double back to reach the chimney. Sparks that come out of the tubes tend to drop instead of making the sharp turn and are thus retained in the smokebox, which must however be long to permit this principle to be applied.

This scheme was tried out in the next Great Western engines built for South Devon service, the 5 ft 8 in. Dukes of 1895. They were basically identical in general form with the Armstrongs, but lacked the dignity bestowed by the larger driving wheels. The extended smokebox of the Dukes did not please every eye, but the extension was made as part of a construction intended to diminish spark throwing; it was a bit of pure utility and whether anyone liked its looks was a matter of no importance whatever. The firebox was flush-topped and some people thought that in this feature the Dukes looked better than the Armstrongs. The Dukes were intended primarily to work on the main line west of Newton Abbot, where curves prohibit high speed even where gravity would make it possible, and so there was no need for them to have 7 ft wheels – nor indeed did any subsequently built Great Western locomotives have wheels as large as that. The 5 ft 8 in. diameter of the Dukes' driving wheels became a Churchward standard as did also the 6 ft. 8 in. diameter used in the next lot of 4-4-os – the Badmintons (W36) built between 1896 and 1900.

4-4-0T NO. I (1880)

By the year 1880 2-4-0 tank engines were common enough and a 4-4-0 tank engine was only a natural development of them. So there was nothing very surprising in the fact that Dean's initial locomotive design for the Great Western should be that of a 4-4-0T (p. 61). A double frame with bunker, backless cab and side tanks was ordinary, although extension of the side tanks so far forward as to reach the smokebox was a bit out of the ordinary and rather damnable in prohibiting top-side access to the mechanism under the boiler. The eye was, however, sharply arrested by the form of the connection – if you could call it a connection – between the bogie and the main frame.

On each side of the locomotive was an E-shaped member with its long side (about 11 ft) horizontal about a foot above rail level. One short side was attached to the buffer-beam and the opposite one to the outside frame plate just ahead of the brake lever in front of the leading coupled wheel. The middle limb was bolted at its top end to the very shallow extension of the outside frame abreast of the rear of the smokebox. From the horizontal limb of this member half the weight of the front of the engine was conveyed through four swing links to tie rods attached to the ends of two laminated springs bearing at their mid-points on the axleboxes. The axleboxes were guided by hornblocks attached to the side plates of a bogie frame.

The front of the engine could thus move laterally in relation to the bogie frame within the increasing restraint of the swing links. By the same virtue the bogie frame could rotate about a vertical axis through a small angle relative to the main frame. And again by the same virtue the bogie could move fore and aft in relation to the main frame although, as no brakes were applied to the bogie wheels, there was no positive tendency to do this.

So without any central pin or corresponding connection with the main frame the front of the engine was supported by a swivelling bogie with gravity-controlled side movement.

So far so good, but to most engineers' eyes the E-shaped members looked frighteningly skimpy. Their limbs were only about 5 in. wide and only ¾-in. thick. The vertical limbs, of which the shortest was 16 in. long, were carrying an average of nearly two tons each. When the engine was standing on perfectly true track this average might not be exceeded, but any departure from truth in the track would alter the distribution of 12 tons total load between the six limbs in a manner affected by the flexibility of the laminated springs.

Laterally the E-members, being very thin, were very flexible, which is not in itself a big disadvantage; but they were also very weak, which meant that excessive speed in running over facing points might bend the E-members permanently out of the vertical plane, although the very flexibility of the arrangement tended to be a safeguard against this.

This examination suggests that the front suspension was not so weak as at first appeared and had probably been very carefully thought out. But it does look as if it could have been so flexible in the lateral sense as to have left most of the guidance of the engine to the flanges of the driving wheels whereas the true function of a leading bogie is to relieve them of that duty.

No. 1 retained her original form for a couple of years but was then altered so that the front was carried by a single axle loaded by laminated springs above the running board. To permit of this the side tanks had to be shortened and this provided the great advantage of permitting some top-side access to the motion. Moreover the increased distance between the crank axle and the preceding axle greatly improved underside access. In her original form No. 1 was very bad indeed in this respect.

In her rebuilt form No. 1 (p. 48A) was a good solid sensible 2–4–oT with a useful life of forty-two years, the last half of which were spent in working mostly between Chester and Birkenhead. In that service she was by far the most capable 2–4–oT and, with slightly extended smokebox, Belpaire firebox and top feed, the most impressive to the eye. One felt that she deserved the distinction of being No. 1 of the Great Western Railway.

4–2–4T NO. 9 (*c.* 1881)

After one has traced with interest some of the very numerous combinations of details in Great Western locomotives of basically simple and prosaic forms, it is startling to come across a drawing of something that is not prosaic and, one would say at first, not very sensible. In this category came Great Western No. 9 of 1881, an extraordinary-looking 4–2–4T standing on a markedly unsymmetrical wheel-base of about 30 ft (p. 62).

Side tanks, higher than the top of 7 ft 8 in. wheels, extended from the cab for 26 ft forward to end 3½ ft ahead of the smokebox. There was a domeless boiler, with flush-top firebox, a backless cab and a bunker about 6 ft long.

Under the footplate and bunker was an outside-frame bogie even more remarkable than those used by Dean to carry passenger vehicles. The official drawing shows a bogie generally similar to that depicted in the official drawing of No. 1, mechanically awkward because No. 9 had no outside frame, but Mr E. W. Twining (in the *Locomotive*, January 1940) showed how it might have been arranged.

Under the smokebox was a group of four solid wheels rather less than 4 ft in diameter. First sight of the drawing suggests that these wheels had inside axleboxes in a bogie frame but closer examination shows no such frame on the drawing; one gains the impression that the draughtsman's attention was distracted just as he was about to add some lines that might have defined a bogie, and he never got back to it.

Mr Twining was inclined to think that the leading axleboxes were in hornblocks attached to the main frames, and not in a bogie frame, on the ground that otherwise the locomotive would have had no fixed wheel base. This is not however quite sound. Those passenger vehicles that were carried each on two of Dean's swing-link bogies had no fixed wheel base but they certainly ran sufficiently well to be kept in service.

Mr Twining remarked that 'No. 9 never did any useful work and was a constant source of trouble owing to its failure to negotiate curves in the yards'. The word 'yards' in this context may perhaps be interpreted as 'works yards' and this leads to the suggestion that the engine never got out on to a running line. Indeed, one asks oneself was the engine ever built? With this thought in mind it is specially interesting to read the following extract from the *Railway Magazine* for November 1908, p. 389. It is part of a serial by G. A.

Sekon on 'Some Links in the Evolution of the Locomotive'. It is composed largely of extracts from the diaries of David Joy linked by Sekon's comments.

Joy reported that, following a discussion at Swindon in 1882 on the subject of possible application of his form of valve gear to a Great Western locomotive he

'. . . saw all about a mighty "single" tank engine Dean and Charlton were building – 8 ft single and double 4 ft wheel bogies at each end. I saw drawings and all, and she looked a beauty. She was intended to do Paddington to Swindon in 2 min. under time and the next one was to have my gear; but the next never came. No. 1 tumbled over the turn-table in going out of the shed, and stayed there covered with a tarpaulin.'

(In this, 'Charlton' is probably a reference to Churchward who was on development work at Swindon at the time.)

Sekon then added:

'When reading the above we thought we had lighted upon a secret chapter in broad-gauge locomotive history; and so we asked Mr Churchward if he could throw any light on David Joy's definite statement. The reply from Swindon, however, not only fails to afford any explanation of Joy's "Swindon ghost" but suggests a very prosaic explanation of the entry in Joy's diary. Mr Churchward's letter is as follows:

'Such an engine as you mention has certainly never been constructed at Swindon. At the time, however, of the amalgamation of the Bristol and Exeter Railway, we took over several engines of the 4–2–4 type and Mr Joy was possibly thinking of these.'

A reader of the *Railway Magazine* wrote in to say that he was certain that a locomotive substantially as described by Joy was built at Swindon, and that it would not run round curves. This information was conveyed to Churchward who agreed, adding that the earlier communication to him had been assumed to apply to a broad-gauge locomotive.

It is interesting to find Joy coupling the name of Churchward (if that name was indeed the one he intended) with that of Dean. It is traditional to detect the hand of Churchward in the experimental designs of locomotive produced in the last few years of Dean's superintendency, but it may not have been suspected that Churchward might have been concerned in some of Dean's early 'flops'.

In 1880 no designer bothered very much about accessibility of the mechanism of a locomotive as he himself was not concerned. Men responsible for maintenance had always had to take things as they found them, and a designer had enough to bother about without worrying about other people's troubles. So the absence of any top-side access to the mechanism of No. 9 may not have been regarded as much of a defect in 1881. The second wheels from the front were so close to the driving wheels that there was no chance for a man of normal size to get between them. No work, such as filling oilboxes on connecting-rod big ends, could possibly be done unless the engine were standing over a pit. By using this pit a man might reach a point from which he could climb on to the cross beam on the front brake levers and by leaning forward and crouching under the boiler he might reach the glands on the piston rods and valve spindles. Dean (or Churchward?) had certainly helped here by placing the Stephenson valve gear outside the frame and outside the driving wheels, so leaving a central space empty.

The valve gear worked valves above the cylinders through rocking shafts and this bit of mechanism had oiling points that, because of the continuous tanks, were very hard to reach. Great help at this point would have been afforded by a transverse tunnel through each tank and abreast of the rocking shaft.

But even apart from operational difficulties in the design as drawn out, the limitation of drive to one axle out of five does not look very sensible if the engine is to pull much more than its own weight up anything like a bank. Nor, having once got going, would the engine be easy to stop with brakes limited to the driving wheels. Only knowledge of the existence and use of the Bristol and Exeter 4-2-4 well-tank engines could have suggested that anything like No. 9 might be worth making at all.

In 1884 Swindon produced a 2-2-2 locomotive to which were attached number plates each displaying the figure 9, although there is certainly no proof that they had ever been attached to an earlier locomotive. The 2–2–2 No. 9, however, did have Stephenson valve gear with eccentrics mounted on extensions of the crank axle outside the wheels virtually as depicted on official drawings of the 4–2–4T No. 9.

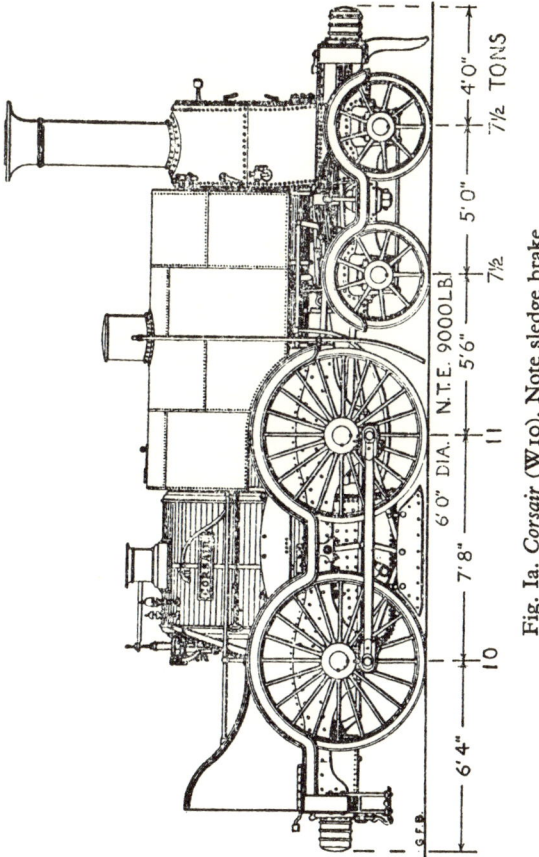

Fig. Ia. *Corsair* (W10). Note sledge brake

57

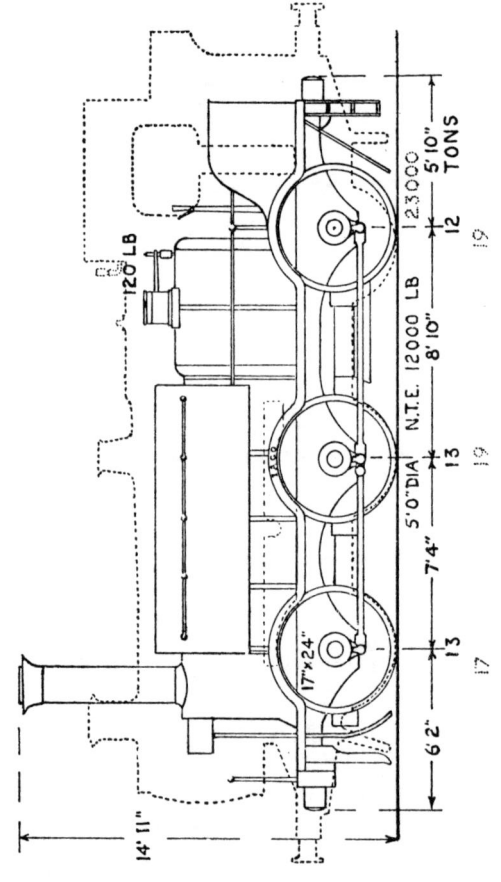

Fig. Ib. *Iago* (W22) built 1852 and 9400 class 0-6-0PT (W81) built 1956

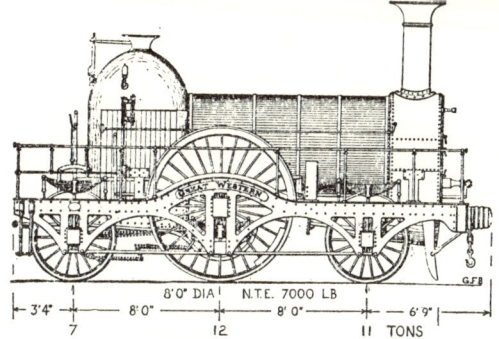

Fig. IIa. *Great Western* (W4) built as a 2-2-2

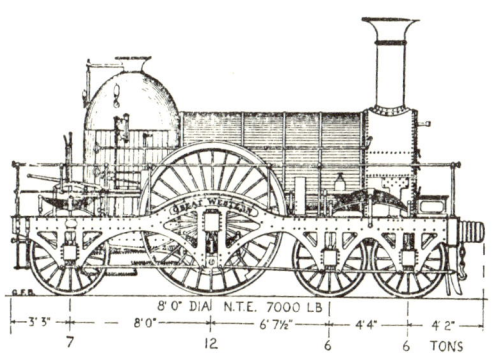

Fig. IIb. *Great Western* (W4) rebuilt as a 4-2-2

59

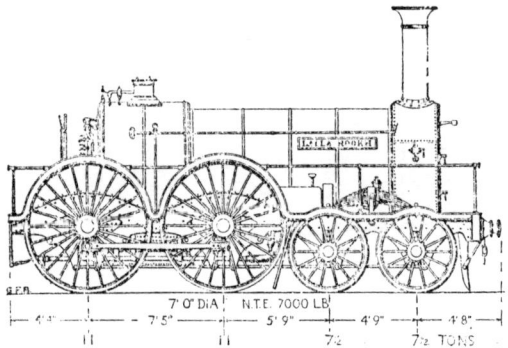

Fig. IIc. *Lalla Rookh* (W12) a 'rigid'-frame 4-4-0

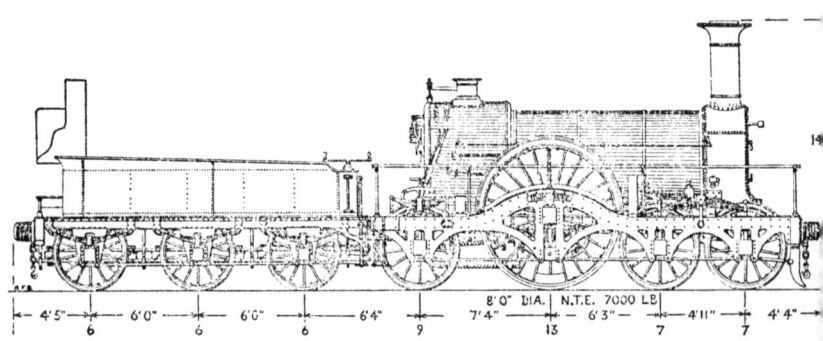

Fig. IId. *Iron Duke* (W6) with 'iron coffin' on the tender

60

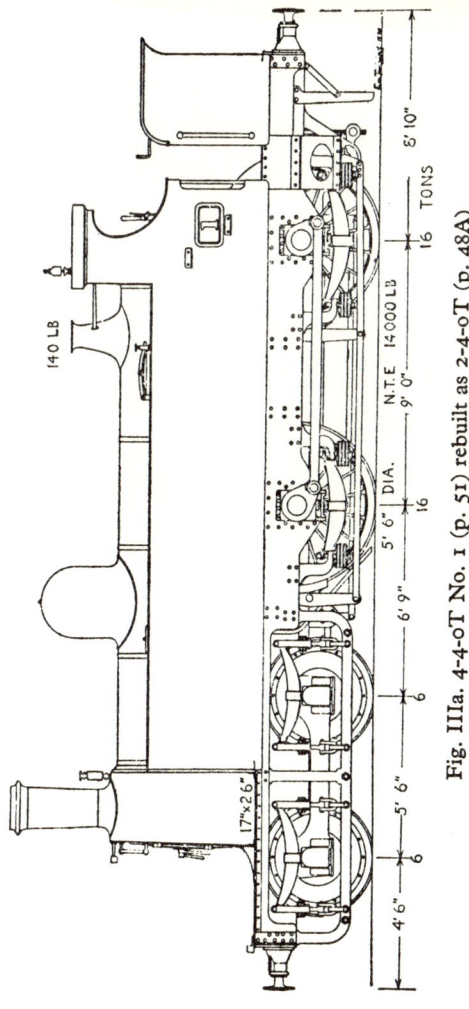

Fig. IIIa. 4-4-0T No. 1 (p. 51) rebuilt as 2-4-0T (p. 48A)

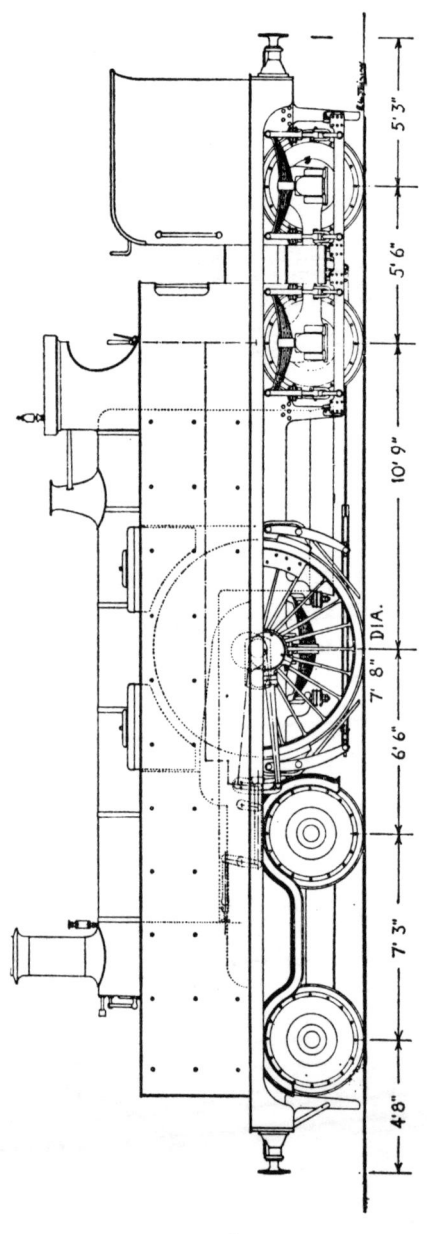

Fig. IIIb. 4-2-4T No. 9 (p. 52). Never any use at all

CHAPTER 3

Dean-Churchward Collaboration

It was all very well for Dean to have let things slide a bit and to have been willing to try anything once. It was all very well for George Armstrong, that tough old bird at Wolverhampton, to rant that what he said went and that he didn't care a damn if he didn't have two engines alike. It was also all very well for enthusiasts to make bets on what boiler No. 936 would have next month, or whether No. 3022 would be running on broad gauge or narrow, or where No. 1137 would be found *when* she was found, but for any approach to peace of mind for Churchward in the twentieth century something more like precision was required. He didn't want to have to *start* wondering what to do when he took charge in 1902; he wanted to have everything sorted out and tested so completely on the design side that any demand on it during his twenty years in the top job could be handled by the office boy.

As Dean's chief assistant Churchward was well placed for persuading him that it might be useful to try out some ideas for bigger and better engines.

The Badmintons (W36) started what was perhaps the most interesting period in Great Western locomotive history. Dean, although approaching retiring age, was experimenting with larger engines – or perhaps it might be more accurate to say that he was authorizing experiments with larger engines, as Churchward was probably suggesting what might be tried. Dean was no doubt anxious to show that he could cope with the situation by introducing bigger locomotives and Churchward was equally anxious to get experiments done and conclusions reached about the proper lines of future development before he succeeded Dean in 1902.

In the Badmintons the raised firebox reappeared, but in the Belpaire form which was used in all Great Western boilers from then on. There were variations in detail in many of the nineteen Badmintons and indeed the last of them, *Waterford*, had a sloping grate cocked over the rear axle, a highly pitched boiler and a long-roofed cab such as never had been seen on the Great Western, but no dome. In fact no more domes were to be made at Swindon for new locomotives. Some would be built on replacement boilers, and brightly gleaming domes would continue to be seen on a couple of thousand Great Western engines for some years to come, but no new design of main-line engine would include a dome.

As it happened, the period was one at which a technical 'step' was being approached. The Armstrong 4–4–0s, with deep firebox between the coupled axles, had a grate area of nearly 21 sq. ft. If much more than this was required, a longer coupled wheel base would be necessary to accommodate a deep firebox of adequate size. To avoid this the grate might be raised above the rear axle but sloped down towards the front. This would be something new in Great Western main-line locomotives.

This feature went into *Bulldog* (W37) in 1898 and remained in all subsequent Great Western 4–4–0s. The sloping grate facilitates firing in that the fuel tends to shuffle itself to the front (lower) end of the grate and this is useful. On the other hand a deep flat grate up to about 24 sq. ft area is not difficult to fire because the drop in the flight of the coal enables the required range to be achieved with lower speed through the fire hole. Moreover the greater depth gives greater furnace-volume.

In 1899 appeared *Waterford* with the safety valves where the dome would normally have been, and in the same year also appeared *Camel* with this feature and also with a cylindrical smoke-box resting on a saddle. The chassis of *Camel* was like that of the Dukes but the boiler and mounting was something new to the Great Western and in an entirely different style. Boiler and firebox looked like a drain pipe glued to a biscuit box and stuck well up in the air in a manner unlike anything created by Gooch or the Armstrongs or previously by Dean, and therefore not liked by many students of the locomotive. Above the gorgeously bitty chassis the engine looked grim and gaunt, a distressing portent of

5a. No. 577 (W24). Note long springs.

5b. No. 3021 (W27) *Wigmore Castle*, derailed in Box Tunnel. This led to rebuilding of the whole class to 4–2–2 wheel arrangement.

5c. No. 3529 (W40). Note jack (for lifting after derailment) on running-board.

5d. No. 3558 (W41). Note reversing rod passing through firebox lagging.

7a. No. 3516 (W30). Stella class.

b. No. 3222 (W31) Barnum class rebuilt with domeless boiler.

c. No. 3222 (W31) Barnum class rebuilt with domed boiler and Belpaire fire-box.

d. No. 16 (W34) *Brunel* rebuilt with domeless boiler.

what was to be expected in future. But this new style of boiler had to be thoroughly tried out because it was much more economical in many ways than the old one.

On the goods side some roughly corresponding experimental engines were built. First was No. 36 (W113) in 1896. This was a 4-6-0, much as one would expect to result from extending the outside frame plates of a double-frame 4-4-0 backwards to accommodate a firebox filling the width between the frame plates and adding a coupled axle to take the weight. The firebox had a raised top but was special in that the grate (area 35 sq. ft) was made in two transverse flat sections with an intervening sloped section. The crank axle was immediately ahead of the firebox and it supported four axleboxes. There were laminated springs throughout engine and tender, nine on each side, as the crank axle had four axleboxes. Some people called No. 36 'the crocodile'.

There was a well-extended smokebox of the usual wrapper-plate type; the official photograph of No. 36 shows very clearly the handle, outside the cab, by which the boiler water gauge cocks could be closed without a hand being placed anywhere near them.

No. 2601 (W114) was of generally similar form to No. 36 but the boiler was more highly pitched and the firebox was of the raised Belpaire type, extended forward to form a 'combustion chamber'. The bogie had an inside frame and the front end of the engine was hung from it by four vertical links arranged in the style of the Dean coach bogie. The leading coupled axleboxes were loaded by nests of coil springs and the other coupled axleboxes by volute springs.

Immediately behind the smokebox was a huge sandbox in the form of a saddle on the boiler barrel. From each side of it a vertical pipe extended down to rail level just in front of the leading coupled wheel. Steps on the smokebox defined a way up to the sandbox.

No. 2601 (dubbed 'Kruger') was followed by nine engines (Mrs Krugers) generally similar except for having a two-wheel leading truck instead of a four-wheel bogie. To the men who had to deal with Nos. 2601-2610 it probably seemed silly to have to hump sand all the way up into the air especially as some of it always managed to trickle down on to the mechanism under the boiler. Authority became convinced of this and the big sandbox was replaced by two ordinary ones but the steps remained. Laminated springs replaced the helical springs on the leading coupled axleboxes.

On the Krugers the Great Western tried single slide-bars, but never again while Churchward was at Swindon. It has been stated that the crank axles were not strong enough and it could be that the 28-in. stroke was a factor here. Certainly it became traditional at Swindon to believe that a crank-throw greater than 13 in. in a crank axle was asking for trouble, but this does not survive rational examination. Quite clearly the life expectation of an axle must be affected by the values of the vertical and horizontal loads on it, and by the thicknesses of its metal.

None of the extraordinary features of these eleven engines survived on the Great Western. The outcome of the experiment that they represented was the Aberdare class 2-6-0 which was in principle the chassis of a normal double-frame 0-6-0 extended forward over a two-wheel truck and carrying a boiler with Belpaire firebox and a cylindrical smokebox resting on a saddle. An intermediate form appeared in No. 33 (W116) on which the boiler barrel was parallel. Aberdares (W117) after No. 2661, were built with taper boilers and all eventually got them.

Starting in 1896–1897 the periodicals *Locomotive* and the *Railway Magazine* were early enough to publish information about developments during this transition period. They must have delighted the locomotive enthusiasts of the time and interested the really 'live' members of the design and development staff at Swindon, but perhaps distressed old stagers who could see no reason for fussing with new things when they knew perfectly well that the old ones were quite all right.

It may be noted that until 1902 all the obviously experimental locomotives built at Swindon had double frames in the Gooch-Armstrong-Dean style and, of course, inside cylinders. The experiments were mostly in the boilers and the Krugers had combustion chambers. This was a strange feature to bother about, as only when exceptionally long-flame coal is burned is there any advantage in providing more furnace-volume than a conventional firebox naturally gives.

So for seven years or so Churchward was inspiring Dean into various carefully contrived experiments with design features that seemed to be working elsewhere in order to find whether they really worked on the Great Western. Churchward had not got *all* the answers by 1902, but in two more years he had established and proved components for an entirely new range of standard locomotives, and these covered not only Churchward's reign but virtually the additional quarter century of the life of the Great Western Railway. His was a famous achievement, unmatched on any other British railway.

4-4-0PT NO. 1490 (W109)

The greatest distinction of this engine is that it was the first on the Great Western Railway to have pannier tanks. It is said to have been devised to supersede the Great Western Metropolitan tanks by something more powerful.

The Metropolitan Railway itself owned 4-4-0 tank engines with outside cylinders over a bogie with wheels nearly touching each other. No. 1490, although also a 4-4-0 tank engine, differed from the Metropolitan engines in every possible way. It is as though someone at Swindon had said, 'Well, we'll set out a 4-4-0T without giving anyone any chance of saying that all we could do was copy what the Metropolitan had been doing for years'.

First of all there were inside cylinders, outside main frame, outside bogie frame, overhung springs, raised Belpaire wide firebox resting on outside frame and wide cab with a good roof.

Tanks were attached to the boiler, with their top and bottom surfaces flush with the top and bottom of the barrel. These 'pannier' tanks did not interfere with boiler mountings or with overhung springs or with top-side access to the mechanism. Why had they never been used before? They did, however, prohibit washout plugs in the side of the firebox at crown-sheet level unless indeed they could be contrived to have adequate capacity without overlapping the firebox.

No. 1490 was not in fact adopted as a prototype for Metro tank engines. The story is that the Metropolitan engineers objected to her weight. There is nothing remarkable about this: they always objected to the weight of any engine that anyone wanted to use on the Metropolitan lines. The trick was to build an engine a bit heavier than it need be, have it rejected by the Metropolitan because of weight, lighten it and offer it again and all was then well. This at least was what was seen to be the case in later years; it may not have emerged by 1898.

So 1490 was tried on other Great Western short-distance passenger-train services but without showing any marked superiority over contemporary engines on the same work. That she had some positive disadvantage is suggested by the fact that she was relegated to shunting work, although she can hardly have been as good as the saddle-tank 0–6–0s at that job. After some time this was realized and as no one could think of any way of rebuilding her to useful purpose (nothing ever beat Swindon works like this!) she was sold in 1907. Her first industrial users (Ebbw Vale Steel, Iron & Coal Co.) did not think much of her, and the Brecon and Merthyr Railway used her only as a temporary stop-gap, but the Cramlington Colliery Co. kept her going, with some modifications, in Northumberland till 1929.

3600 CLASS 2–4–2T (W55)

Great Western short-distance passenger trains had been handled well for many years by 2–4–0Ts and 0–4–2Ts but towards the end of the nineteenth century a need was discerned for something larger and a fairly obvious move was to the 2–4–2T. Tank engines of this type were already in extensive use on the North Western, North Eastern, Great Eastern and Lancashire and Yorkshire Railways. Their symmetrical wheel arrangement seemed obviously right for engines that normally ran equal distances forward and backward and so something of this kind was at least worth trying.

So in 1900 No. 11 was built in conventional style but with a raised Belpaire firebox in accordance with the current Great Western boiler fashion at that time. Two years' trial of No. 11 was sufficiently encouraging to warrant the building of twenty similar engines (Nos. 3601–3620) in 1902, although it is perhaps a pity that they were not made exactly the same as No. 11.

Churchward was, however, experimenting with piston valves at the time and fitted all but one of this batch of engines with 6½-in. double-ported piston valves instead of the conventional flat valves used in No. 11. Normal practice in inside-cylinder engines is to place piston valves either above the cylinders or below them. In the 3600s, however, the piston-valve centre lines were in the central longitudinal plane of the locomotive, the valve for the right-hand cylinder being above it and that for the left hand cylinder beneath it.

The valves were worked by Stephenson gear as used in No. 11 but with oblique offsetting arms to reach the valve spindles. These valves did not give satisfactory service and in about six years the cylinders were replaced by others similar to those of No. 11. In 1903 a second and final batch of engines (Nos. 3621–3630) were built to the original design with flat valves.

In later years these engines were fitted with coned boilers of the No. 3 standard type substantially the same as No. 2 but with a shorter barrel and in due course with superheaters.

The class was limited to thirty-one engines because by 1904 Churchward had started his lines of 2/2–6–2Ts which more than covered the abilities of the 3600s and were built of his new standard components.

In accordance with immediately pre-Churchward fashion at Swindon, the 3600s had steam brakes and steam-operated reversing gear. They also had steam operation of two-way water-scoops, but the vent-pipes on the tanks were not big enough for high-speed pick-up of water. This was demonstrated by No. 11 when picking up from a trough near Rowington Junction (between Hatton and Lapworth on the Leamington-Birmingham line). The water rose so rapidly in its tanks that the pressure of air above became so great that they burst. Repetition of this type of accident was avoided by fitting much larger vents under mushroom-shaped covers.

The 3600s were primarily intended for suburban services from Paddington and Birmingham but they were to be found over the years in other localities, for example between Chester and Birkenhead. They had all been withdrawn from service by 1934, having been superseded in most places by 2/2–6–2Ts of the same design as those which, by their appearance in 1904, had made the 3600 design obsolete.

69

The Armstrong and Dean passenger-tank engines were lively little creatures and the 3600s could be just as bright. On an occasion noted in the *Railway Magazine* for November 1918, No. 3611 pulling 150 tons ran from Slough to Paddington, 18·5 miles, in 19 minutes 40 seconds start-to-stop, averaging 59 m.p.h. from Langley to West Drayton, 65 thence to Southall, 68·6 on to Ealing and 65·5 from there to Westbourne Park. The time of 2 minutes 8 seconds over the last 1·25 miles was one second slower than that of *Tregenna Castle* at the end of her record-breaking run from Swindon in 1932. No. 3611 ran in from Southall in 9 minutes 8 seconds which may be compared with the 10½-minute allowance for the Cheltenham Flyer and the Bristolian before World War II.

THE BIRDS (W48)

If one finds the appearance of a locomotive – or of anything – attractive, is there any reason for telling anyone else about it? Is it not possible that he will think that you are bothering with something that is no concern of his? On the other hand, is it possible that he may now find in looking at a picture of that locomotive a pleasure that he might not otherwise have had?

I was always fascinated by the appearance of double-frame locomotives and my liking for them was not at all diminished by the fact that they were easier to draw freehand than inside-frame engines, because only small arcs of wheel rims could be seen. Drawing circles or ellipses without mechanical aid is unrewarding work.

But even among double-frame locomotives some looked better than others because of their general form, the setting of their boiler, and other details. I believe that the Dean 4–2–2s were favourites and so perhaps were the Armstrong 4–4–0s. Certainly I preferred the latter, partly I suppose because a 4–4–0 is a more sensible engine than a 4–2–2 which does not use much of its weight to grip the rails.

When double-frame 4–4–0s began to come out of Swindon works with highly set boilers in what was later recognized to be a Church-ward style, some critics were appalled as they could see only ugliness in this development. The severe rectilinearity which was apparent in the side view of the early Bulldogs' boilers did later give place to a slightly softened version in which the rear ring of the barrel was tapered so that it joined the raised firebox with rather less of a jolt. Nevertheless, even this type of boiler mounted over 6 ft 8 in. wheels in the Cities looked rather gawky, and certainly the Cities lacked the elegance of the Armstrongs. They looked indeed a bit top heavy, and the side view hardly suggested a flyer. In fact they were not top heavy and one or two of them at least *were* flyers.

The smaller wheels of the Bulldogs enabled the boiler to be set lower in the Cities and this, together with a longer extension of the smokebox, gave the last lot of Bulldogs (named after birds) an appearance which to my mind was superb. I would not say that it was magnificent, but it was perky in a graceful way. The aggressive set of the smokebox and the solid depth of the outside frame suggests a lively locomotive, strong in its essential guts. The wheels were discreetly hidden but the springs were there for all to see. The boiler was not too high and the locomotive looked long rather than lofty. The Churchward boiler and the Dean chassis were blended in a beautifully vivacious combination of the old and the new. It was as though Churchward, with his new designs well launched to dominate the next thirty years and more, specially built ten engines with one of his best boilers on a final development of the double-frame 4–4–0 as a salute to the work of Dean in the nineteenth century.

Built in 1909–1910 the Birds were not large engines: they were intended for secondary services and they had no need in the ordinary way to display high power or high speed. They looked as if they could be lively and it is good to be able to quote times and speeds recorded by Mr C. J. Allen in a 200-ton train running from Swindon to Oxford behind No. 3451 *Pelican*, one of the last five Birds to be built.

The train passed Steventon, 20·8 miles from the start, at $72\frac{1}{2}$ m.p.h., having averaged 71·2 m.p.h. over the ten miles down at about 1 in 750 from Uffington. Then, as so often happened, there were checks in the approach to Didcot and the train took nearly 39 minutes to the stop at Oxford, 34 miles from Swindon.

This was in 1929 when photography was not very advanced and many worthy railway subjects could not be precisely recorded in moving multicolour. How heartwarming it would be to see a colour film of *Pelican* flitting down the famous speedway with copper-rimmed chimney, green boiler, brass-rimmed name plate and flashing crank webs! There would be no need to over-speed the presentation on the screen; the right speed would be good enough.

Such reproduction is not practicable but in this book we get as near to it as is possible in static black and white by reproducing on p. 144B a very fine photograph by Mr M. W. Earley of *Skylark* heading a Stephenson Locomotive Society special in 1951.

On the Bluebell Railway in Sussex there is a 3200 class Dukedog 4–4–0 which in its lower parts approximates to a Bird, and Great Western admirers are glad of it; but it is no longer practicable for any double-frame 4–4–0 to match the gay flight of *Pelican* down the Vale of White Horse.

Mr Holcroft has stated that the Birds were produced to meet an immediate need for more locomotives for secondary services. Churchward adopted what was an outdated design simply because he had not decided what was to be his modern design for that class of work. When he did decide, his choice (4300 class 2/2–6–0) was so clearly the obvious one that double-frame enthusiasts must thank the vacillation that led to the birth of the Birds.

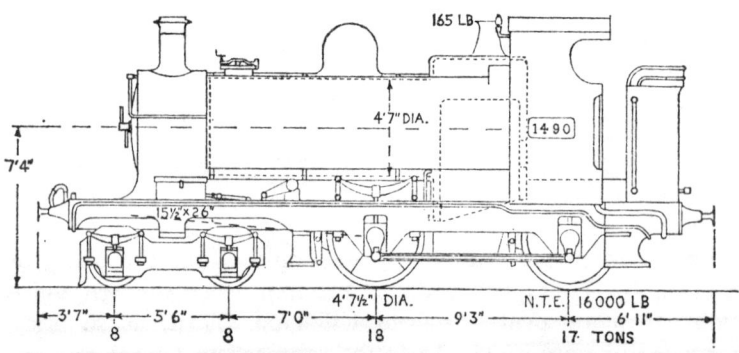

Experimental tank engine No. 1490 (W109)

CHAPTER 4

Churchward Alone

During the twentieth century the solid achievements of Great Western steam no less than the dramatic ones have fascinated enthusiasts and have caused many of them almost to worship the man responsible. Admirers have called their houses 'Churchward'; one discussion in a technical journal on the subject of locomotive valves and valve gear ended abruptly when a contributor referred to him as Jackson Churchward – name dropping of that order stunned everyone. Interest in the work of Churchward locomotives led to interest in their origin, in what was done at Swindon, and in how it was done. What kind of man was it who directed such successful development?

A notably undramatic one! Born and raised at Stoke Gabriel within earshot (on a still evening) of locomotives on the South Devon Railway, he was attracted by the possibility of getting a job in connection with them. This he did, at Newton Abbot, and having shown all the useful qualities he was transferred in 1876, at the age of nineteen, to Swindon after the Great Western had absorbed the smaller company. There, by working hard and studying form and doing the other right things he gained such promotion and experience that in twenty years he could see that the top job was within his reach and that with a bit of common sense and initial energy he could make most of its twenty-year tenure pretty easy. His career was not one of darting about hither and thither getting wide experience in many fields but rather of sticking around and being on the spot when jobs were being reshuffled. He took an active interest in civic affairs and at the age of forty-one became the first Mayor of the Borough of the newly amalgamated Old and New

Swindon. He has been rightly praised for his foresight, tact and knowledge of human nature. He appreciated that in explaining a situation very clearly to the boss it is better not to have a wife and family to support. (These circumstances are, of course, modified if the wife also has a job.) He was fortunate in that, during the last few years before the retirement of Dean, whose supreme position Churchward was clearly to get, Dean suffered from premature senility and offered little resistance to having his hand held. He was therefore rather easily persuaded to undertake experiments that Churchward wanted to make in order to clear the ground for developments that would enable him to sit back for his last ten years as the head of Great Western steam.

All this worked out beautifully and Churchward soon had his organization streamlined smoothly with plenty of bright young men delighted to do the work and encouraged by him to show what they could do. Everyone knew where he was, including Churchward. With no domestic worries and his way to retirement pretty clear he could be to the staff a benevolent figure rather than an autocratic one. At home he tended his garden like any suburban householder and at weekends, being interested and skilled in shooting, he had many a crack at the birds.

The few anecdotes related about Churchward are astonishingly naïve. They are characterized by his use of the universal adjective 'bloody' and, it would seem, necessarily so. Take 'bloody' out of a Churchward anecdote and no anecdote remains. Great man of perception and action though he undoubtedly was when it came to words Churchward was no Churchill.

It would of course have been more remarkable to be told that the word 'bloody' had been used by, say Francis Webb at Crewe, who had been born and bred in a vicarage, while Churchward was raised on a farm, and it is interesting to think of the two great railway towns of Crewe and Swindon, in each of which the bachelor head of mechanical engineering was also the civic head. One of them would neither say 'bloody' nor smile, whilst the other could do both at once. It may be admitted, however, that to survive Richard Moon and the North Western three-cylinder compounds with jollity would have required something like a combination of Drummond, Churchward and Bob Hope.

The word 'bloody' was probably used frequently by Church-ward and not merely in anecdotal circumstances. It was probably common enough in all phases of his activities, not even excluding meetings of the Urban District Council. It may even be the case that to omit the word from a Churchward anecdote would be to convey an incorrect impression.

Among the many interesting details of Churchward's family history is the existence of the motto *Ales Volat Propitiis*. One may imagine this to be translated by Churchward as he aimed his gun at some bird that had caught his destructive eye as 'This'll propi-tiate your (bloody) flight, birdie'.

An oft-quoted story about Churchward relates to his response to a directorial complaint that Great Western locomotives cost more to build than did North Western contemporaries. He is said to have remarked in extenuation that 'one of mine can pull two of their bloody things backwards'.

If he did say this and really meant it, he may have had in mind two very small 'bloody things' such as the tiny 0–4–0Ts that worked on the narrow-gauge system in Crewe works, or perhaps he meant (without saying so) that the bloody things were opposing no deliberate resistance to being pulled.

The remark in fact is too vague to have any meaning. To admit of positive statements the case may be considered of a GW Star coupled tender to tender with a 1904 Precursor itself coupled behind a similar Precursor all on dry level rails.

Consideration of adhesion weight, nominal tractive effort and normal coefficient of friction enables one to say that:

(1) if either side had all its brakes on, the other side would not be able to move it, and
(2) if each side did its best to run chimney first the two North Western engines would succeed and the Star would fail.

This of course was obvious to Churchward. He could be quite sure that it would not be obvious to any ordinary director, who could therefore be satisfactorily blinded by a bit of dramatic piffle whose only strength lay in the 'bloody'.

But perhaps the anecdote was never intended to be examined technically. When it first appeared in print, the word 'bloody' snatched the breath of every reader. It is hard to think that any

75

combination of six letters would do so in the 1970s and so future references to this incident will probably be made only by those who have come to believe that the adjective used by Churchward was not in fact quite so respectable as 'bloody'.

But in no anecdote or any more solidly authenticated account of any of Churchward's doings is there any hint that he was other than a universally admired and universally respected chief of a large department and civic head of a dual town. His occasional descents from dignity were benignly human and added to his stature. He was a great man and a great head of all his men.

At least one of his decisions came in for some extra-mural criticism about twenty years after it was made. The Great Western naturally wished to take a prominent part in the Railway Centenary celebrations to be held at Darlington in 1925 and the first thing was to consider what historical relics might be exhibited. Then it was remembered that what would have been absolutely right for this purpose were Gooch's *North Star* of 1838 and his *Lord of the Isles* of 1851, which had been preserved in Swindon works till 1905, when they were scrapped by Churchward. Locomotive archaeologists are apt to think bitterly of this, but perhaps they forget that in 1905 Churchward was still building for the future and a locomotive was for him just something to be used if it *could* be used and to be scrapped if it couldn't.

'Never look back' is still approved advice to ambitious young men and in 1905 Churchward was only forty-eight. 'History is bunk' is a remark made by Henry Ford so long ago that it is now bunk itself but Churchward may have had Ford's attitude in 1905.

The poet Horace declared himself to have raised a monument more abiding than brass but even brass is not markedly abiding in the civic sulphur of today and steam locomotives being largely ferrous are even less so. Preservation of locomotives therefore demands sheltered space and in Churchward's time Swindon works were demanding more of just that same thing.

Every astute manager will tell you that efficient progress requires 'cutting out the dead stuff' and dramatic action of this kind is a managerial status symbol. If the material of the dead stuff is used again, that warrants an additional merit award. It may well be that some of the material of the original *North Star* was used in

76

building one of Churchward's Stars which in time showed themselves to be locomotive lords of the British Isles.

The 1925 centenary officials were not so impressed with Churchward's memory as to believe that what he scrapped should remain scrapped. So it was announced that a replica of *North Star* would be built and an appeal was made to borrow any surviving bits. Many such bits were retrieved and it became apparent that *North Star* had not been scrapped so much as dismantled. Among the parts that remained were the driving wheels and crank axle. It looks as if either Churchward had not had the heart to declare that as Swindon works was limited to about 300 acres they could not find room for a pair of wheels or that the wheels had been kept out of his sight.

The replica was exhibited not only at Darlington in 1925 but also at the Fair of the Iron Horse in the Baltimore and Ohio Railway Centenary in 1927. This was staged at Halethorpe, Maryland, a suburb seven miles out from Baltimore and the first Great Western King class 4/4–6–0 was also present.

Churchward's life ended while he was following up a report he had made in December 1933 about a defect in one of the main line tracks near to his house. Because of one of those absurdities that seem inseparable from large organizations, a bit of repacking of sleepers just outside Swindon works could not be officially done until the message sent from there had trickled through an office forty miles away and such trickling can go on for days. The job was a little one when someone got round to it, but in the meantime the condition of a rail joint was deteriorating with the passage of every train. On one of his regular crossings of the main line Churchward paused to examine the joint while deafness prevented him from perceiving the approach of a train through fog. He was killed on the spot with out warning and to few is Fate so merciful.

In February 1922 the *Railway Magazine* had paid Churchward a compliment:

'It would be invidious to suggest that Mr G. J. Churchward, C.B.E., who retired from the position of Chief Mechanical Engineer of the Great Western Railway, is the greatest locomotive engineer in modern British practice.'

Praise of this kind is not uncommon in funeral orations and the like but this was outstanding in being published while he was alive.

DEVELOPMENT BY CHURCHWARD

Some enthusiastic students of British railways or British locomotives confess (or even proclaim) that they have no interest in the railways of foreign countries. This is not a cause for criticism for, after all, their is no compulsion on anyone to be enthusiastic about anything.

Some British locomotive engineers may similarly have lacked interest in engineering on foreign railways. This was no ground for criticism (except perhaps by a discerning general manager) but it was not wise.

G. J. Churchward, having lived his working life in the service first of the South Devon Railway and afterwards of the Great Western Railway, could have been excused for believing that methods used on the latter railway were probably as good as those used anywhere else and that they could continue to be employed in conditions that changed only slowly. He did in fact study – to a greater or lesser extent – locomotive practice in other countries and certainly the countries nearest to Devon in the east-west sense, i.e. France and America.

He had grown up with locomotives having crank axles and in many cases double frames, both expensive components of a locomotive, and had no doubt become so used to them as to overlook their unsatisfactory characteristics. Many other British railways had also to cope with the manufacture and maintenance of such things, but in America they were very little used (if at all) and to some engineers perhaps quite unknown. As the Americans were clearly able to 'get along' without having to tolerate these hindrances, were we in Britain really sensible in accepting them? Had not the Stephensons been a little precipitate in abandoning the Rocket layout in favour of a double frame and inside cylinders instead of studying the former a little more closely? The character of early American railway track made it essential for each of the early locomotives to have a 'track-feeler', i.e. a two-wheel truck that, running ahead of the locomotive proper, could convey by spring pressure on the main frame some guidance in the direction that would soon be demanded by the curvature of the track. Such guidance could restrain the locomotive from swaying about a vertical axis as she ran along the track. Why had we not done some similar thing here? This was only an academic question in 1895. The real point was that the Americans were successfully using locomotives of much simpler construction than was normal on the Great Western. We had followed an artifice adopted by the Stephensons to avoid a difficulty in the running of four-wheel engines with outside cylinders and the artifice was still being followed in eight-wheel engines and would soon, unless someone woke up, be followed in ten-wheel engines. Yes! six-coupled wheels would soon be necessary under main-line passenger-train engines and as a bogie is needed for safe running at high speeds, large-wheel 4–6–0s were going to be needed, perhaps not immediately but almost certainly before Churchward retired at the end of 1921. So the obvious thing for him to do was to see whether the Americans had got round to 4–6–0s for fast passenger trains. If they had their designs would be worth studying. So after looking through engineering journals he might well have found such a picture as that of No. 891 (p. 96A) which represents a typical American 4–6–0 of the early twentieth century, not a bit the kind of thing they were currently turning out of Swindon or indeed out of any of the works of any British railway at the time.

He would have been less shocked than some other British loco-motive engineers might have been by the complete exposure of the wheels because that was a feature of many of the broad-gauge engines. He would ignore the cow catcher as being superfluous in Britain since British cows were persuaded by walls, hedges and barbed wire to keep away from railway trains and he would ignore the cab as in England it never became so cold as it always did in North American winters. He would see the smokebox in the form of a drum resting on a curved saddle that looked as if it could have been made in one piece with the cylinders and valve chests. He would notice that there was absolutely nothing to stop the lid of the valve chest from being lifted right off after the studs had been taken out. No nonsense about having to pull the bogie out before you could get at the valves! And of course there was no crank axle.

Although the picture does not show it clearly he would guess that the main frame was made from steel bars about 5 in. square in section, welded or bolted together.

There would be no difficulty in making something like this for the Great Western Railway, apart from the bar frame (which would be new for Swindon) and that could easily be replaced by a plate frame.

To make the smokebox saddle, cylinders and steam chests in one piece would mean a very big casting and that might be difficult or even impracticable, but to make the right-hand and left-hand halves separately and bolt them together was reasonable and would make, perhaps, a better job.

The design of such an engine would be prepared on a clean sheet having no trace or hint of existing Great Western designs. There would be no playing about with an old engine and working out how to fit her with a new boiler and new cylinders and new frame and new wheels to make her into a flyer. No! It would be pleasant to start from scratch and to design an easily-built engine that would meet the Great Western main-line passenger train needs not only now but for some years ahead. If at the same time the main-line passenger-train engine could be built of components that might also be used in engines for other jobs, that would save a lot of time and money. So the first job was to visualize all the demands on the Locomotive Department until 1922 and to plan a range of really standard locomotives that would meet them. There would, of course, be some spots of bother in 'getting the bugs out' of the prototype engines and this might take a year or two to do, but after that Churchward could have about fifteen years of peace so far as locomotive design was concerned, and so would have more time to devote to the less tractable parts of the boss's job.

What an easy and even attractive job it seems to be, to start with a clean sheet and to outline a number of different designs built from standard components! Any locomotive engineer would have been glad to do this, one would think, confident in the knowledge that it would lead to economies in the end. There is evidence that Churchward did it in 1901 and that British Railways did it in 1948–1950, but there is nothing positive in respect of other railways.

The job is not so easy as it looks at first as the clean sheet soon becomes soiled. The rail gauge, the loading gauge and the structure gauge have to be marked on it and they cut down the area of the clean sheet to something quite small. Permissible axle loads have to be ascertained from the civil engineer and this is not as easy as one might think. It has to be decided what shall be the minimum radius of track curvature for which the locomotive shall be designed. It has to be decided what is the maximum sustained power to be expected from each locomotive at each of a range of speeds. It has to be ascertained what will be the limitation of machining capacity and lifting capacity in the works when the first locomotive of each class is to be built. For each problem in detail design it is useful to know what solution has been used by the designers of successfully operating locomotives elsewhere.

So even if one starts from a clean sheet in developing a new series of locomotive designs it does not necessarily mean the job will be an easy one, even when basic principles in design are all cut and dried. The cautious designer may well doubt whether it is safe to base on cut-and-dried principles in designing things that will be expected to cope with conditions twenty years ahead. Even if those conditions can be closely predicted, what new basic principles may have been proved in the meantime to be advantageous? Sixty years after the Rocket triumphed at Rainhill, steam locomotives in common use were in essence either Rockets or Planets, Stephensons' immediate inside-cylinder versions of Rockets. Could nothing better be made?

In 1901 Churchward was asking himself questions of this type. What about using the compound expansion principle? No designer of large stationary steam engines or of large marine engines would ask this question. Compound expansion – in two, three or even four stages – was accepted as normal. Compound expansion locomotives were being used on many railways. It was true that the Great Western Railway itself had had two compound 2–4–0s – Nos. 7 and 8 – and had not made any sense out of them. It was true that the North Eastern Railway had built considerable numbers of two-cylinder compound engines but was now rebuilding certain classes of compound engine into the ordinary (non-compound) condition. It was true that the London and North Western Railway had built large numbers of compound engines and it was clear to the intelligent observer that some at least of these engines were pretty poor things. These circumstances offered no encouragement whatever to the belief that compounding of steam locomotives was markedly beneficial.

On the Northern Railway of France trains running regularly at booked average speeds of over 60 m.p.h. were the fastest in the world at the time and they were hauled by four-cylinder compound locomotives. This did not really conflict with British evidence about the value of compounding but it did suggest that compounding was not bound to be bad. It *was* bound to introduce some complication into the locomotive and so the real question was, 'Can the possible advantage of compounding in saving a bit of coal be equalled by designing simple (single-expansion) engines rather more carefully with that end in view?' In other words, 'Are we doing the best that we might in our designs of non-compound engines?'

It would have taken some years to answer that question properly and Churchward could not wait. So he went ahead on the basis of simple engines with the hope that in a year of two someone would find out how to make them as thermally efficient as compound engines. In the meantime they were mechanically superior because they were, or could be, mechanically simpler.

A possible source of worry in standardization is that some development in technique soon after the general scheme has been prepared may suggest that some things might have been better done differently. An example of this was the development of a sound method of superheating in the years 1901 to 1905.

Another example was the sudden American acceptance of Walschaerts valve gear just after Churchward had frozen new standard designs including Stephenson valve gear which had up to then been universal in America. If Churchward had waited for three or four years he might have standardized rather better designs than he actually did.

Churchward recognized in the first instance three possible types of traffic distinguished by differences in average running speed and therefore, in principle, suited by three different driving-wheel diameters.

	Selected wheel
Service	diam. (in.)
Express passenger	80½
Mixed traffic	68
Goods and mineral	55½

This early decision on wheel diameters was very valuable. There was never any real need to use any wheel diameter other than these but alas! after Churchward had retired, his clear-sighted rigour also retired and thinking methods tended to become as vague as they seemed to have been in other locomotive design departments. In every organization in which standards have been set up there is an anti-standardization clique whose prime object is to see them knocked down by finding apparent reasons why they cannot be used. The clique at Swindon had the wit to keep quiet so long as Churchward was on the job. Some of the subsequent fiddling at Swindon with piffling departures from the Churchward standard wheel diameters demonstrated either bloodymindedness or sheer lack of thorough technical understanding.

The task Churchward set himself was to decide how big the biggest standard boiler would need to be. The next item was to outline the design of an American-style 4–6–0 that could use, economically, the full output of that boiler over the normal range of running speed, on the level and up ordinary gradients of the trains that the engine would be required to handle. He decided that an American-style engine should have a piston stroke that was American rather than British and chose 30 in., longer than that used in any British locomotive other than W. Bouch's Ginx's Babies, 4–4–0s built for the Stockton and Darlington Railway in 1871.

Being convinced that a high ratio of piston stroke to cylinder diameter helped in getting a high cylinder efficiency he chose 18 in. as the cylinder diameter. He believed that a boiler pressure of 200 p.s.i. would suffice in such cylinders to give as much tractive effort as was needed in the near future, and the same castings could be bored out to 19½ in. if that should become useful. His first choice of 6½ in. as the diameter of the piston valves showed that Swindon had not yet got really down to the rational dimensioning of piston valves. Indeed at the time it had not produced really satisfactory piston valves at all. To find a way of doing so was an urgent practical problem on which work was already in progress. The solution eventually adopted by Churchward was to use the semi-plug type of valve devised in America.

Although coned boiler barrels were common enough in America Churchward did not specify one for the first experimental engine; but he used the principle soon afterwards, standardized its application and made the taper boiler a noticeable Great Western speciality in Great Britain.

American practice was to place the valves above the cylinders and to work each valve by Stephenson gear and a rocking shaft extending laterally through a gap in the bar frame. This was simple and convenient as the gaps in bar frames were large.

The same arrangement was hardly practicable with plate frames, because the plate would be too seriously weakened by a hole big enough to permit easy mounting of the rocking shaft. So Churchward mounted the rocking shaft with a pendant lever at each end, above the top edge of the frame plate and used an inclined 'extension rod' to connect the link block to the lower end of the inner lever on the rocking shaft.

Extension rods and valve rods of different lengths were required for different classes of locomotive, but the eccentrics and expansion link were common to all classes and remained as unchanging standard components of Great Western locomotives for over sixty years.

Use of the cylinder-and-half-saddle construction prohibited the use of frame plates extending throughout the length of the locomotive. In Churchward designs, the frame was basically of the inside type and extended from the cross plate at the back of the engine to the rear of the cylinder casting. From there extension frames bolted to the frame plates reached forward under the cylinder casting to the buffer beam.

The slide-bar brackets extended upwards and were stiffened by attachment to a plate stretching across the frame and curved at its top edge to lie within half an inch of the similarly-shaped underside of the boiler barrel. The plate formed a cradle that supported the front end of the boiler if and when either cylinder block was removed from the frame. Cylinder castings used to get damaged by sidelong collisions at the junctions in running-shed yards and after such incidents it was useful to be able to dismember the front end of a locomotive without disturbing the boiler.

The extension frames look a little weak in this frame structure but it was used in Churchward's first 2/4–6–0s and then adopted as a standard. It was applied in all of the hundreds of Churchward two-cylinder locomotives built over the ensuing forty years.

A simple, strong, straightforward construction had thus been devised for a two-cylinder engine but was that sufficient? A sensible compound engine would need at least three cylinders. Need compounding be considered seriously? What was the result of considering whether a single-expansion locomotive can be designed and built to attain almost the highest efficiency to be expected in a compound locomotive?

A purely paper exercise based on knowledge well proved long before 1900 could have shown that the greatest possible amount of useful work from steam working past piston valves into and out of a locomotive cylinder is obtained:

(a) when the cut-off is in the range 15 to 25 per cent (with about 10 per cent clearance volume), and

(b) when the running speed is within a particular range determined by the ratio of the product of driving-wheel diameter, valve diameter and valve lap to the cylinder volume.

So in designing for minimum coal consumption when developing some specified power at any speed within a certain range, the procedure is:

(1) to use a combination of boiler pressure, cylinder volume and driving-wheel diameter as to develop the required power at the middle of the specified speed range with about 20 per cent cut-off, and

(2) to use such a combination of valve diameter, valve lap, cylinder volume and driving wheel diameter as will ensure that the valve may admit to the cylinder all the steam that it can take in the specified operating conditions.

Whether this type of calculation was made at Swindon is not clear, but it might have been. Whether it were done or not, it would be very sensible to try out the conclusions derived from the calculation in a steam engine. This *was* done at Swindon. A small stationary engine was built for the purpose of demonstrating the effect of varying valve dimensions and thus providing positive guidance in valve design.

One thing that was bound to have emerged from any investigation of this character was that for an 18-in. cylinder, a piston stroke of 30 in. and a wheel diameter of about 80 in. a flat valve about 18 in. wide with the usual lap of about 1·25 in. could do what was wanted only over a speed range of about 20 to 40 m.p.h. This was not high enough for main-line passenger trains and so a much bigger valve was necessary, but a flat valve much wider than the cylinder would be difficult to accommodate in a conventional steam locomotive. Piston valves were, on this account, a must in the fast main-line engine primarily in mind. No particular design of piston-valve had been proved at Swindon at the time but at least it could be calculated how big it should be.

To achieve high cylinder efficiency over the range 40 to 80 m.p.h., a cylinder 18 × 30 in. requires the product of valve diameter and valve lap to be about 15 sq. in. For example, a 10-in. valve needs 1½-in. lap or an 8½-in. valve needs 1·75-in. lap. In his first general scheme for new standard locomotives, Churchward specified 6½-in. valves but the lap (equally important) was not mentioned.

Either a 10-in. diameter or a 1·75-in. lap would be outside general experience in Britain and perhaps that was why Churchward thought it might be useful to avoid both these dimensions by using a valve that opened double ports. It would have two admission edges on each head and so a 6½-in. double-ported valve was equivalent to a 13-in. valve working in the ordinary way on a single line of ports. Although there was something dubious about this, valves of this type were provided in Churchward's first 2/4–6–0 No. 100 which began running in 1902.

The technical staff were naturally interested in the performance of these valves and so indicator diagrams were taken to get information on this point and also to find to what extent steam pressure

86

contributed to the noticeable knock in axleboxes. This was the first big outside-cylinder locomotive the Great Western had ever had and everybody was surprised at the severity of axlebox knock when things had worn a bit slack.

At the same time investigations were continued on the performance of valves of different dimensions fitted into the stationary steam engine specially built for the purpose.

An intermediate conclusion was that No. 100 would do better with bigger valves and it was found possible to get $7\frac{1}{2}$-in. valves into enlarged bores in the cylinder blocks. Further tests were run with these valves and they did better than the smaller ones. After examining all the available information, however, it was decided that while the $7\frac{1}{2}$-in. double-ported valves performed well enough for them to be retained in No. 100 for use in the ordinary way on fast main-line trains, 10-in. single-ported valves would be superior and should be used in future locomotives in the new standardization scheme. As usual in steam locomotives, simple size was more practical than ingenious gadgetry.

So the second 2/4–6–0– No. 98 was given 10-in. piston valves of simple design with 1·75 in. lap in the cylinder-and-half-saddle construction described above. In this locomotive all the essentials were right and she was the prototype of the class of 77 2/4–6–0s that came to be known as the Saints.

CHAPTER 5

Development of the Saints

⤚⟡⤜

ALBION AND THE ATLANTICS (W107)

Soon after No. 98 started running a very similar engine, No. 171, was built and its safety valves were set to blow at 225 p.s.i. because its performance was to be compared with that of the French-built compound Atlantic *La France* which used steam at 227 p.s.i.

The name *Albion* given to No. 171 was clearly appropriate and especially because conversion from 2/4-6-0 to 2/4-4-2 in 1904 and reconversion to 2/4-6-0 in 1907 suggested an impermanence in line with the traditional perfidy of Albion. The first change was to make the engines more closely comparable in everything except the simple/compound diversity; the change back was an indication that Churchward had reached a decision about the comparison between *Albion* on the one hand and the French compounds (*La France* and Nos. 103 and 104, set to work in 1905) on the other.

In 1905 and 1906 Swindon built thirteen Atlantics generally similar to *Albion*, easily convertible to 2/4-6-0s in case that should turn out to be desirable. It did, but it was not done till 1912.

For general purposes a 4-6-0 is superior to the corresponding 4-4-2 because of the markedly extra nominal adhesion and because of the further extra associated with the effect of the drawbar pull in transferring vertical load from the leading axle to the trailing one. But in 1904 six-coupled engines for high speed were novel and there was a feeling that frictional losses in the extra crank pins might make a 4-6-0 perceptibly less free in running than was the corresponding 4-4-2. There seems in fact to be no evidence that the effect was more than minute, whereas the gain from greater adhesion weight was very marked when the need was to pull hard.

Apart from *Albion* and *Lalla Rookh*, the Great Western 2/4–6–0s that had started life as Atlantics were identifiable by the fact that their names were titles of novels by Sir Walter Scott. Most of the names had been used on the Gooch broad-gauge 4–4–0s of the Waverley class built by Robert Stephenson & Co. in 1855. Six 2/4–6–0s (Nos. 173 to 178) built in 1905 were named after current directors of the Great Western Railway.

A major factor in determining the height of the boiler when a 4–6–0 is being designed is the height of the rear axle, because the local bit of the ashpan and the grate have to be higher still. A number of different designs of British 4–6–0s were unsatisfactory largely because the grate was starved of air; in keeping the boiler down as low as possible the designer had underestimated the engine's need for air.

No mistake of this sort had been made at Swindon in respect of the 2/4–6–0s. The ashpan had an adjustable air inlet at the front, another at the back and two under the ashpan arch over the rear axle. (See p. 114.)

When it came to designing the ashpan for the Atlantics the problem was easier, because the ashpan was lower but less care was taken over the matter, and the Atlantics in consequence did not steam so well as the 2/4–6–0s. This was very puzzling till someone noticed the Atlantics' disadvantage in air-access to the fire and Churchward admitted that the point had been underestimated in the beginning.

But even fifty years later designers were still failing to realize that ashpans were apt to have ash dropped into them and that if that went on too far it would throttle the engine unless the ashpan were properly designed. Anyone could calculate the nominal tractive effort of a locomotive, but nobody calculated what weight of ash would choke it.

Before the end of 1905 it had been concluded that the compound engines had, on the whole, no superiority over the Great Western engines and, more main-line engines being required, ten (Nos. 2901 to 2910) were built which were generally similar to *Albion* in her original condition as a 2/4–6–0, and started regular work in March 1906. These engines were named Ladies (W84), a piece of admirable originality that was perhaps not widely appreciated at the time and may indeed have been thought incongruous by those who had tried without success to distinguish any elegance in the lines of the locomotives. Led by a *Lady Superior* these engines had an aspect of rectilinear rigour that did not persist in Churchward designs and was, for example, absent from his later Birds.

No. 2901 was distinguished in being the first British locomotive to be built with a fire-tube superheater of the Schmidt type. In recognition of this and in conformity with current practice her maximum boiler pressure was at first limited to 200 p.s.i. instead of the 225 p.s.i. of the 2900 class. Then after two or three years there was a reshuffling of boilers and in the course of this No. 2901 lost her superheater for a time.

There was no uniformity in the boiler barrels or the smokeboxes of Nos. 2901–2910 as built. Some barrels were in the form of a short cone and a cylinder; others were long cones united to short cylinders. Eventually all the Standard No. 1 boilers had barrels uniformly coned over the whole length and were joined to long smokeboxes.

Before she was properly run-in No. 2903 *Lady of Lyons*, had touched about 120 m.p.h. in coming back to Swindon from Stoke Gifford on a trial trip without a train. This was not announced at the time and it appears from reluctant admissions over twenty-five years later that it was an unofficial effort made to satisfy one or more of the officials riding on the footplate. The impression one forms is that no hint of this episode was allowed to reach Churchward beforehand.

No. 2903 also distinguished herself later by taking a test-train from Paddington to Plymouth (225·7 miles) by the Westbury route in 225 minutes and also in running from Paddington to Exeter inside 3 hours, taking 440 tons to Westbury, 360 to Taunton and 283 to Exeter.

To reverse a Lady or to readjust her cut-off careful handling of a tall reversing lever was required; (in Swindon works they spoke of the lever as a pole). This seemed inappropriate and perhaps risky on a fast locomotive of this size, especially as Dean had applied screw reverse to Great Western locomotives much earlier than this, and indeed steam reversers were fitted to some double-frame 4–4–0s and to the Aberdares. The fact was that, remarkably enough, American practice had not really advanced beyond lever-type reversing gear when Churchward was first thinking about big 2/4-6-0s, and he was thoroughly sold on American practice at the time.

Furthermore, although screw reversing gear was used in all the 2/4-6-0s later than the Ladies, nevertheless lever reverse was standard on the equally large 2800 class 2-8-0s and on the larger 4700 class 2-8-0s.

By the end of 1906 it had become clear that these Churchward 2/4-6-0s were the best main-line passenger train locomotives in Great Britain. They could pull heavy trains at well over the required speeds and had confirmed in ordinary service the impression created by No. 2903 that they were flyers. All Great Western men were pleased with them and proud of them as fast workers, but not everyone liked the look of them. The small highly-perched cabs, the steel steps leading up to them, the abrupt drop at the front end of the high running board and their general aspect of being undressed distinguished them unfavourably by comparison with other British locomotives. Contemporary new locomotives on the Great Central Railway, for example, were quite different in these (purely superficial) respects.

DOUBLE-FRAME LADY

Churchward and Dean between them did a lot of experimenting with different boilers whilst retaining the Great Western general styles of double frame and inside cylinders. This was very sensible; to alter many things at once, whilst superficially saving time in experimentation, can be misleading. In 1902 whilst the outside-cylinder arrangement was still on trial, appeared the first of the City class 4-4-0s (W44) with what was almost exactly the eventual No. 4 standard boiler on something like the Atbara 4-4-0 chassis (W43). Churchward might well have considered extending this to a 4-6-0 if his outside-cylinder designs had looked like being slow in getting off the mark. He might indeed have considered an inside-cylinder equivalent of the Ladies, that is, a Dean double-frame 4-6-0 with a No. 1 standard boiler. The diagram on p. 100 shows how such an engine might have appeared; it would have been heavier and constructionally more complicated than the actual Ladies but it could just have happened. The name shown would have been an appropriate reference to its development and origin.

Consideration of ratio of connecting-rod length to piston stroke within a reasonable spacing of the bogie centre and the driving axle restricts the stroke to 26 in. and the cylinder diameter then has to be 20 in. to correspond to the $18\frac{1}{2}$ in. of the Ladies.

The cylinders can be set parallel to the rails without restricting side movement of bogie wheels 7 ft apart, and so there is plenty of room for 10-in. piston valves above the cylinders without raising the boiler above Lady-height.

The most attractive valve gear is the Stévart cross-connected Walschaerts, successfully used for twenty-four years in Churchward's first four-cylinder engine, because it has no eccentrics. A more extensively-used alternative, with that same advantage, is Joy valve gear but only the North Western and the Lancashire and Yorkshire liked this very much.

The wheelbase of this long Lady is 2 in. shorter than that of the King and the coupled wheelbase is 18 in. shorter.

THE SAINTS

Although the primary concern of railway directors may not be the company's technical possessions, directors may be personally interested in locomotives and may not like to think that their own company's locomotives were inferior to those of other companies. So it is very likely that questions were asked at board meetings or at the associated luncheons about the relative beauty of Great Central Atlantics and Great Western 2/4–6–0s and 2/4–4–2s. At all events something was said somewhere, and as a result Mr H. Holcroft, then a member of the technical staff at Swindon, was asked to consider possible methods of softening the visual angularities of the 'twenty-nines' as more were going to be built and it was desired that they should look as if somebody at Swindon had bothered about their appearance.

Mr Holcroft soon showed that the side view of a twenty-nine lost its crude angularity and its general appearance enormously improved when a couple of circular arcs were added in the right places. On the engine itself this meant the addition of a curved plate extending right across the width of the buffer beam, just ahead of the valve chests, and a downward extension of each cab side sheet to an extra curved bit of running board.

This modification was entirely in the style of the Great Central Atlantics and 4–6–0s and so might be expected to mollify those who thought that the Great Western should be able to match its neighbours on all counts. It was adopted in August and September 1907 in building twenty 4–6–0s generally similar to the Ladies, but improved by having reversing screws instead of reversing poles. These engines were numbered 2911 to 2930 and were named after Saints.

Between September 1911 and May 1913 twenty-five similar engines were built and these were named after Courts and numbered 2931 to 2955.

The 2/4–4–2s built in 1905 were rebuilt as 2/4–6–0s and with *Albion* and the 2/4–6–0s built between 1904 and 1906 had their numbers increased by 2800 and then formed a group numbered 2971 to 2990 inclusive. The original 2/4–6–0 No. 100 was renumbered 2900 and the second 2/4–6–0 No. 98 was renumbered 2998.

All these engines were colloquially known as Saints or twenty-nines. They were not all alike in every detail but only No. 2900 had any real mechanical difference from the others.

The diagrams on p. 98/9 are intended to show the development of the boiler and front end of the Saint from an elemental 2/4–6–0 and also to demonstrate the importance of the length of the smokebox and the position of the chimney in determining the external character of the locomotive.

In I the boiler is a rectangular box with a cylindrical barrel; the smokebox is long enough to take the chimney and no more.

In II the smokebox has been slightly extended, the dome suppressed, the running board lowered and splashers added for the driving wheels.

In III the boiler barrel is tapered over part of its length.

In IV the boiler barrel is tapered over its whole length and the smokebox has been lengthened.

In V circular-arc drop ends have been added to the running board.

In VI the chimney has been moved to show how easily a locomotive could be made to look horrid.

After 1924 the Great Western built some 470 2/4–6–0s of designs differing only slightly from that of the Saints. The LMS class 5s, LNER class B1s and British Railways classes 4 and 5 2/4–6–0s numbered some 1350 locomotives of designs that can be traced back to an origin in the Saints. This first Churchward design established the 2/4–6–0 as an admirable express-passenger-train locomotive, the directly derived Great Western Hall proved it as a mixed-traffic locomotive and nothing better for that purpose was devised in the whole history of steam on the railways of Great Britain.

GENERAL COMMENT

Churchward's standard components, boilers, cylinders, wheels, motion and axleboxes were employed in over 1100 Great Western locomotives other than 2/4–6–0s. In addition the 5600 class 0–6–2Ts, numbering 200 locomotives, had a Churchward standard boiler and most of the valve gear was of the Churchward standard design. After Churchward retired, the Great Western built over 1200 pannier-tank 0–6–0s which included nothing of Churchward design apart from the tanks; all but ten of them were basically of Dean design.

It is not too much to say that apart from what there was new in the 1500 class 2/0–6–0PTs built in 1949, no really new design work was necessary in the locomotive department of the Great Western Railway after 1908 when Churchward's Star class 4/4–6–0s had been proved in service. The fact that thus he covered a great railway's tractive requirements for forty years ahead was a convincing proof of Churchward's grasp of the design side of his job and also of his successors' recognition that he really had grasped it.

Before gasping too deeply over this and asking why 'no less than' should not have been inserted before the word 'forty', the reader may pause to reflect that forty years was not a very long time by railway standards. Forty years elapsed between Trevithick's Pen y darren locomotive and the attainment of a mile-a-minute by steam. The broad gauge was in full swing for over thirty years.

Locomotives were expected to last for at least thirty years. Train-heating boilers in diesel locomotives had not been made reliable in twenty years.

Victorian rates of development in technology were breathtaking compared with what had been achieved over the preceding centuries of civilization but they themselves have been surpassed to the extent that in modern times any new design of aircraft, for example, may be out of date before the prototype has been tested.

Such disconcerting instability had not been a feature of development of the steam locomotive after about 1840, if at all. Progress during the latter half of the nineteenth century was quite slow, with the Great Western lagging rather than leading. Even Churchward, as part of his monumental fresh start in design, took one big backward step, and this merits notice for more than one reason.

REVERSING GEAR

Pole reversing gear

Perhaps the most extraordinary feature in Churchward's design practice was the use of a reversing lever (or 'pole') instead of a reversing screw on biggish engines that had to run fast. With a pole reverse it was risky (on most big engines) to try to make a small change of cut-off when pulling at speed as disengagement of the detent from the notch that was locating the lever might allow it to be pulled into full gear by the engine against the greatest resistance that any average driver could apply. So normal practice was to start in full gear and to stay there until the engine was running at about 15 m.p.h., to close the regulator, to pull the pole quickly back to the driver's favourite notch, and then to set the regulator to suit the needs of the current situation. Variation of effort during the journey was normally made by variation of regulator opening; change of cut-off was usually effected only at a low speed with the regulator no more than slightly open. This seems very primitive to those who have read of Castles and Kings careering along with cut-off varied by only 1 or 2 per cent at a time, but it did not prevent the very numerous Churchward locomotives with pole reverse from doing excellent work. Indeed the virtually fixed cut-off might persuade a driver to let his engine keep on pulling harder than he

95

would have permitted if he could have reduced the cut-off by reasonable procedure, such as rotating a screw.

Any locomotive with Stephenson valve gear or Walschaerts valve gear when running and pulling would set itself in full gear, given the slightest chance. In America this offence was known as 'nose-diving'. Screw reversing gear was the safest in this respect as it restrained nose-diving to a gradual descent. Defects in power reversing gear could lead to sudden complete loss of grip and the engine would then nose-dive and if running fast would start to heave her fire out of the chimney with an alarming roar. The driver had then to turn on the blower, close the regulator and then do what he could to get the cut-off back to where he wanted it.

In view of the dangers in the nose-diving of big engines it is surprising that Churchward applied pole reversing gear in some 550 full-size locomotives, including his largest, the 4700 class 2/2–8–0s.

A diagram reproduced (on p. 101) from a booklet by E. J. Nutty on 'GWR Two-Cylinder Piston-Valve Locomotives' shows that the pole stood between two quadrants notched to give eleven cut-off settings in forward gear and eleven in backward gear. In the range from 22 to 39 per cent the steps are so short that the notches would have to be uselessly narrow and weak if made in a single quadrant. So two quadrants were used and the pole carried a sliding detent for each of them. Operation of the latch lifted both detents; release of the latch allowed one or other of the detents to drop into a notch while the other rested on its quadrant.

The official cut-off for running with only 'drifting' steam was 45 per cent and each relevant notch was identified by a cross stamped on each side of it.

The quadrants carried no numerical indication of cut-off. Such indication would not have helped the driver even if it had been correct, and it would not have remained correct in service even if pains had been taken to get it right in initial erection.

Screw reversing gear

The reversing gear applied by Churchward to the Saints was nicely placed to enable the driver to exert his full strength on the

a. No. 3258 (W35) Duke class, *King Arthur*.

. No. 3312 (W37) *Bulldog*.

No. 3310 (W38) *Waterford*. Driver preoccupied.

No. 3306 (W37) *Armorel*. Long smokebox.

9a. No. 2227 (W56) County tank.

b. No. 4600 (W112). Only one of its kind.

c. No. 4560 (W95) Note recess for upper rear lamp-iron.

handles. They were at about chest height and were well behind the boiler back, so that the driver could get in line with them to pull on one and push on the other if they should prove hard to shift. This was excellent, but it meant that the support for the screw was just where the driver would place himself to look out of the front window. It compelled him, therefore, to give his spine a north-easterly curvature, which became known as the 'twenty-nine bend', but at least he had something to lean on except perhaps when the riding was very rough. (See p. 171.)

It turned out that it was only rarely that the screw and the mechanism were very tight; in general it was not difficult to rotate the handle. So in 1914, halfway through the production of the 4046–4060 batch of Princesses, the reversing screw was moved forward so that it was partly outside the cab, and the driver could stand behind the handles. In that position he could turn them – because they were not usually hard to turn – with a stirring-pudding action and the twenty-nine bend condition disappeared.

One may be quite sure that some drivers complained that they had now nothing to lean on, but the new position was adopted as standard although there was no planned alteration of existing twenty-nine benders.

By the time the first Castle was being built in 1923 it was realized that the new position of the reversing screw left room for a tip-up seat for the driver. So he got one, and so did his mate who would otherwise have complained.

Power reversing gear
To anyone who ever saw an engine driver have a series of struggles with a reversing lever or a reversing handle during shunting operations it was obvious that with all that power available in the boiler some could be spared to relieve the driver of that type of toil.

Many British railways acted on this suggestion and tried steam reversing gear but in no case did any of them go in for widespread application of such mechanism. In every case a trouble was that as the engine ran the cut-off gradually moved slowly or quickly towards full gear. In few cases was it possible for the driver to use power reversing gear to attain any desired cut-off setting with any approach to precision. In no case did it matter because the setting would change anyway.

The Great Western fitted steam reversing gear to a number of locomotives in the early 1900s (the Aberdare class, for example) but with the usual unsatisfactory results. So post-Dean general practice on the Great Western was to use screw reverse or pole reverse.

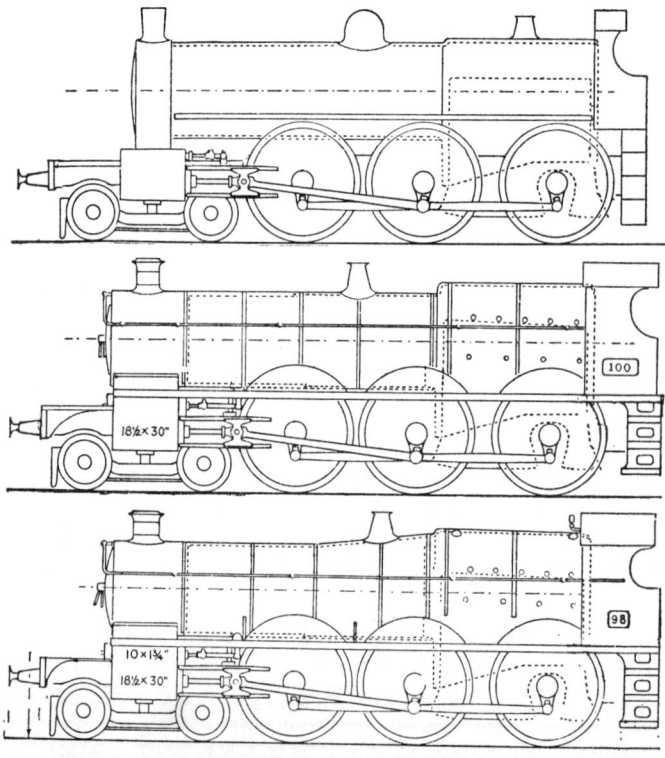

Fig. IV. Stages in development of Saint

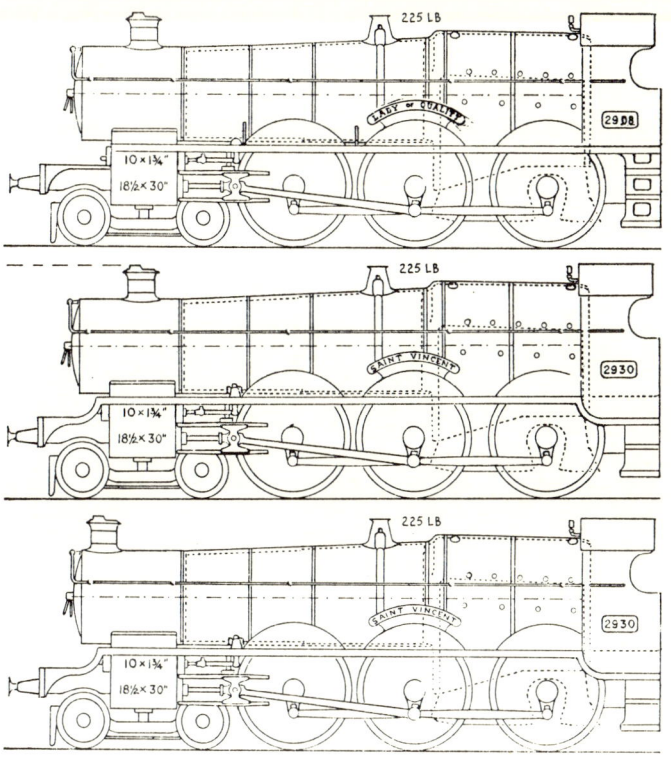

Fig. IV *cont*. Stages in development of Saint

An oddity of Churchward 2/4-6-os was that the pin-connection between the front coupling rod and the rear one was ahead of the main crank-pin and therefore hidden by the connecting-rod.

99

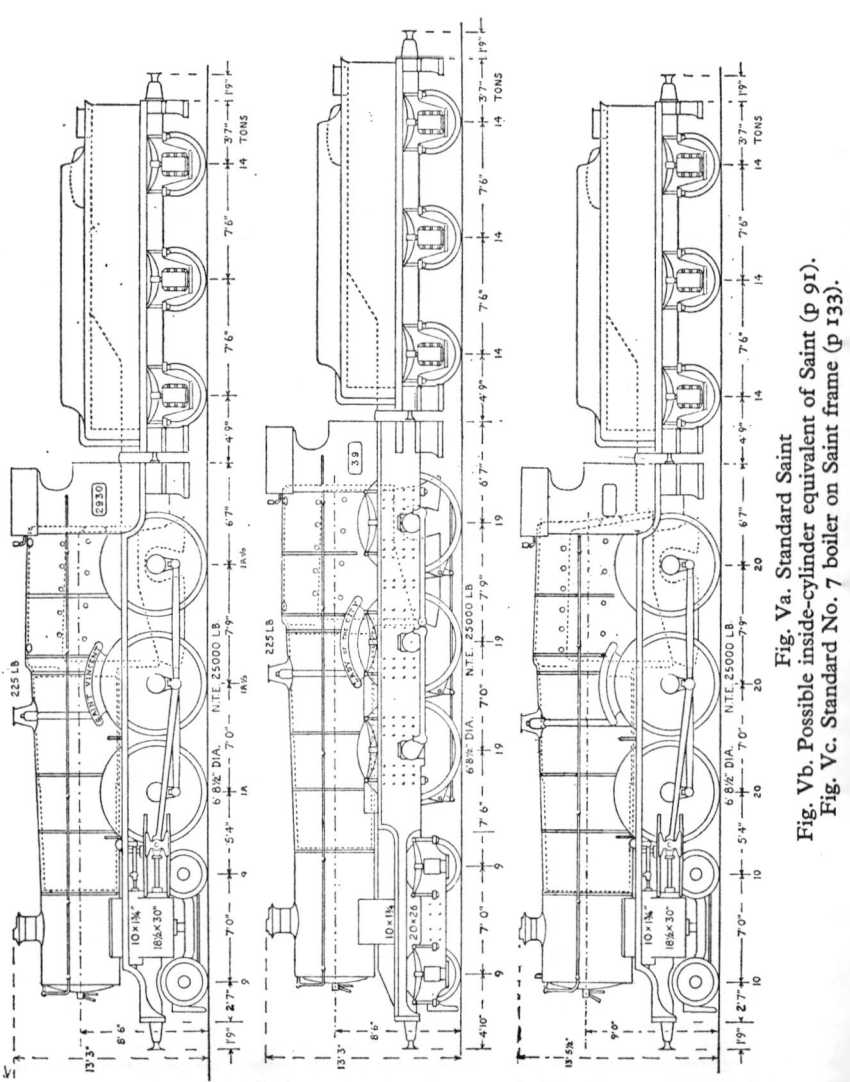

Fig. Va. Standard Saint
Fig. Vb. Possible inside-cylinder equivalent of Saint (p 91).
Fig. Vc. Standard No. 7 boiler on Saint frame (p 133).

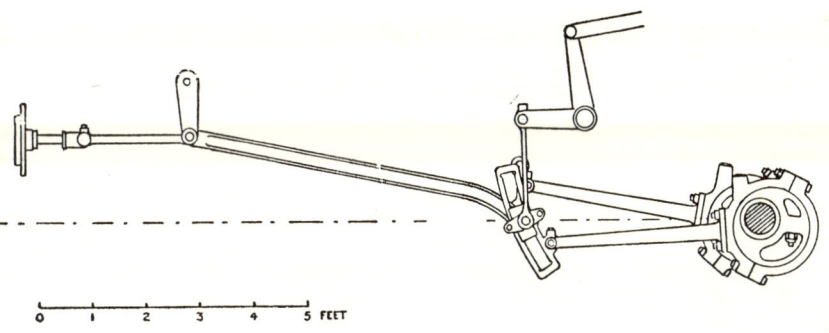

Fig. VIa. Valve gear of Saint (p. 84)

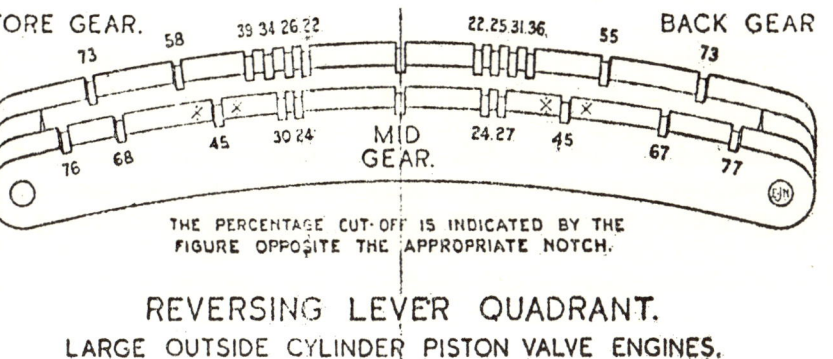

FORE GEAR.
BACK GEAR

73   58   39 34 26 22   22. 25. 31. 36.   55   73

76   68   45   30 24   MID GEAR.   24. 27   45   67   77

THE PERCENTAGE CUT-OFF IS INDICATED BY THE
FIGURE OPPOSITE THE APPROPRIATE NOTCH.

REVERSING LEVER QUADRANT.
LARGE OUTSIDE CYLINDER PISTON VALVE ENGINES.

Fig. VIb. Quadrant for reversing-pole in Ladies (p. 96)

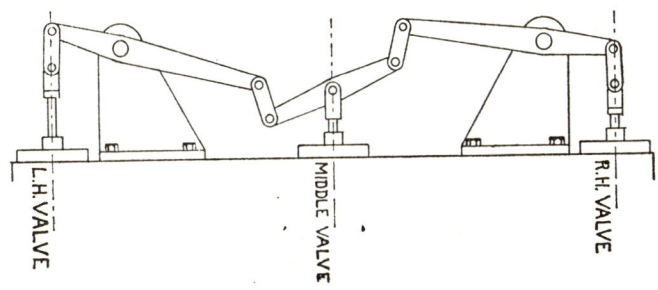

L.H. VALVE   MIDDLE VALVE   R.H. VALVE

Fig. VIc. Holcroft conjugating mechanism (p. 141)

101

CHAPTER 6

Saints in Service

Here the word 'Saint' is used to identify all the Churchward 2-cylinder 4–6–0s, and not merely the twenty examples that bore Saint names. It is certain that this form of locomotive was introduced on the Great Western for main-line passenger-train service and this includes the haulage of heavy trains at high speed. Although the Saints met all Great Western needs in this respect, the contemporary Star class four-cylinder 4–6–0s were still most commonly used on the best trains and these were in general the hardest jobs. The reason for this was that the Star was a smooth-riding luxury model and before World War I the railways could – just – afford a few luxury models characterized by having more than two cylinders each. Between the wars the four railway groups were unanimous in having luxury models defined in this way. After World War II tradition retained the same policy but nationalization of railways in 1948 ended it, and no further pretence was made on the point: the nation could not afford to spend money on luxury-model locomotives. Two-cylinder Pacifics would be used for the heaviest passenger trains but two-cylinder 4–6–0s would cover the bulk of main-line passenger trains and the fitted goods trains. This would provide long-term confirmation if any were needed that the Saint when first built was a general utility main-line locomotive that would meet a great many needs for forty years ahead. Over all those forty years, however, the Great Western continued to feel that it could afford to run luxury models in the form of enlarged Stars and to run them in such numbers as to cover all the heavier and faster passenger trains. There was consequently no special scope for 2/4–6–0s in such service; Great Western locomotives of that description need not be designed for the top speeds. According to indestructible tradition they could therefore have smaller driving wheels and so Swindon built no more 6 ft 8 in. 2/4–6–0s after Churchward's retirement.

The Ladies and Saints showed immediately that they could pull and run to cover all current Great Western requirements with plenty to spare. Some enginemen were convinced that the Saints ran more freely than the Stars and some confirmation of this is to be found in very much later information, derived from test-results, about internal resistance of Great Western two-cylinder and four-cylinder engines. The inevitably rougher riding of the Saints tended to discourage engine-men from letting them go as fast as they might but it is interesting to recollect that Mr C. J. Allen's first note of 90 m.p.h. was when travelling behind *Saint Bartholomew* on a Birmingham-Paddington express at Denham. There seems to be no record of any higher speed than this by any 2900 in ordinary service.

When it came to slogging at moderate and low speeds, most enginemen preferred Saints to Stars, and the differences in valve/cylinder proportions can suggest a possible reason for this. The speed range for highest cylinder efficiency in the Saint was 42 to 84 m.p.h., whereas the corresponding range for the Star as built with $14\frac{1}{4}$-in. cylinders was 65 to 130 m.p.h. or with the later 15-in. cylinders 58 to 116 m.p.h. So at 45 m.p.h., for example, the Saint could be working at highest cylinder efficiency whereas the Star was not. At, say, 30 m.p.h., below the best speed ranges for both classes, the advantage of the Saint over the Star was even more marked.

In most steam locomotives, running normally, steam began to be admitted behind a piston to push it during a stroke just before the completion of the previous stroke and if this were overdone there would be knock and a tendency to overheat the big ends of the connecting rods. This effect increased with shortening of cut off and it was much more marked with Stephenson than with Walschaerts valve gear. It fixed a minimum comfortable cut-off in any particular engine at any particular speed. Very broadly, a Star might be run at a nominal cut-off of as little as 13 per cent whilst the minimum for most Saints was about 22 per cent. This is sometimes quoted to the disadvantage of the Saint on the basis of the false assumption that the earlier the cut-off, the higher the cylinder efficiency. That is not the case. Cylinder efficiency hardly varies from its maximum anywhere in the range from 15 to 25 per cent.

The Churchward standard Stephenson valve gear gave negative lead in full gear. This was an unavoidable consequence of designing the gear so that it would give satisfactory valve events at cut offs down to 22 per cent. Churchward did not seek it but it has been claimed to be advantageous when starting from rest in full gear. There is, however, very little in it, as its effect is exercised only when the piston is very near to the end of a stroke and in that circumstance the crank angle makes it impossible for the piston load to make any perceptible difference to the tractive effort.

After Churchward's retirement the Saints were gradually modified in detail to conform to current standards. The pipes that led steam from the superheater to the cylinders were brought out of the smokebox at the greatest convenient height in order to minimize clutter inside it. Shorter chimneys and shorter safety-valve covers replaced the original ones; this was a well-known way of making a locomotive look bigger.

The lower part of the illustration on p. 160A shows the last surviving Saint shortly before withdrawal from service in October 1953, after having run more than two million miles. Each coupled wheel has a web between the spokes adjacent to the crank pin; this was a feature taken from late LMS practice. The main springs have sagged and would, in the ordinary way, have been readjusted to bring the centre line of the cylinders up to the height of the centre lines of the coupled wheels.

Ahead of the leading splasher can be seen the edge of the cradle which is there to support the front part of the boiler if and when the cylinders are taken off.

Below the chimney is a casing over the oil pipes where they come out from under the boiler lagging plates and are joined to connections with oil pipes in the smokebox.

The nearly vertical outside steam pipe from smokebox to valve chest is a late Churchward feature in that he applied it to the large-boilered 2–8–0s of the 4700 class in the last year of his office at Swindon. The first use of such pipes on a Saint occurred in 1930 when that historic flyer No. 2903 *Lady of Lyons* was so fitted.

Naturally no locomotive was modified in this way before the cylinder casting had to be replaced for one reason or another.

Prominent on the right-hand side of a Saint was the air pump driven by an upward-reaching arm on the crosshead. Churchward is said to have refused to use any unsymmetrical crosshead because the inertia forces on it would impose alternating bending moments on the piston rod – yet he accepted markedly offset air pumps which certainly produced bending stresses on piston rods. (It is said that the LMS abandoned crosshead-driven pumps because they caused piston-rods to break.)

One consequence of using valves large enough to feed the cylinders properly at speed even with travel reduced to give 22 per cent cut-off was that there was plenty of port-opening to exhaust. This was made very clear by the explosive exhaust sound from any Churchward engine when starting from rest or running slowly.

To the emotions these deep detonations were most stimulating (it is a pity that no sound-recording technique has reproduced them) but the fierce draught caused coal lifted from the fire to play hell with the plates and stayheads in the fireboxes of locomotives that did a lot of slow hard pulling. So alleviation was sought by departing from the ideal of short exhaust passages tapering gradually from steam chest to blast nozzle. Mr Holcroft has described how he devised an arrangement whereby steam was exhausted into the very large volume of the smokebox-saddle casting and came out through the blast pipe, reduced (it was hoped) in vigour. In actual fact the effect of this change was imperceptible and while this was disappointing to the engineers it must have been good news to enthusiasts who had become fond of those glorious bangs. The Stars, with longer exhaust pipes, could not quite match them.

Because of its fewer working parts, a Saint was less expensive to build and to maintain than was a Star engaged on similar duty. Only the Great Western authorities could obtain any reliable information on this point. Nothing was published about it, but the outside observer is free to make what deductions he likes from the fact that in the later days of the Great Western Railway its four-cylinder 4-6-0s were well outnumbered by its two-cylinder 4-6-0s.

The heaviest regular work of the Saints in passenger service was done between Newport and London in the late 1920s before any

Castle class locomotive had been stationed at Landore. With the heaviest trains (which occasionally exceeded 500 tons) they were assisted between Severn Tunnel Junction and Badminton but could battle on from there to London in 100 minutes for the 100 miles. A notable feat of No. 2902 on one of these occasions was to sustain 73 m.p.h. on the level with 485 tons.

The work of the Saints west of Newport was far less extensively documented than was their work between there and London and so some notes made by the late Mr G. H. W. Clifford on this subject are specially welcome. Page 192 relates to a run of the morning Paddington-Fishguard boat train well before World War I, on an occasion when it was nearly a quarter of an hour late in leaving Cardiff. About half the lost time was recovered by running the $44\frac{1}{2}$ miles to Landore in $47\frac{1}{2}$ minutes. There are severe undulations in this route, besides a speed restriction to 60 m.p.h. at Bridgend and one to 30 m.p.h. at Neath.

A speed of 65 m.p.h. was sustained for some distance between St Fagans and Llantrisant and the sharp rise at 1 in 106 to the summit at Llanharan did not bring the train below 52 m.p.h. The maximum speed below Pencoed was 80 m.p.h. The minimum speed at Stormy Siding was 48 m.p.h. but any passenger leaning out of a window must have found it very much more stormy at Margam Moors where 90 m.p.h. was touched.

Formal speed restrictions were reasonably well observed and the ardent running elsewhere should have pleased everybody except perhaps the fireman.

Recovery of railway speeds after their depression during World War I began on the Great Western in 1921 and there was another step up in 1923. At about this time Saints on 2-hour expresses from Bristol to London were occasionally noted to be sustaining speeds of 80 to 83 m.p.h. on the level stretches east of Didcot and this kind of running assured the authorities that they could safely schedule a Saint to take the 270-ton Cheltenham Tea-Car Express into Paddington, 75 minutes after leaving Swindon, 77·3 miles back. This the Saints did very easily and within a year the very oldest true Saint, No. 98, then No. 2998 *Ernest Cunard*, was once observed to stop at Paddington with an eight-coach train from Bristol, 62 minutes after passing Swindon. In due course (about eight years) this kind of running led to the 65-minute start-to-stop schedule of the 'Cheltenham Flyer' between those points. By then Castles worked this train and in doing so commonly ran at 90 m.p.h on the level. It is not known whether any Saint ever did this or ever ran the train at all on the 65-minute schedule.

But even when there were plenty of four-cylinder engines to work the flyers there were opportunities for Saints to show what they could do. An example quoted in the *Railway Magazine* for November 1936 was the exploit of No. 2937 *Clevedon Court*, in running from Reading to Bristol after replacing a King that had got into early difficulties in working the down Bristolian. The seven-coach train of 216 tons was of course a featherweight for a Saint and the driver did not spare her. The result was that the 82·3 miles to Bristol were covered in a net time of 69 minutes start-to-stop at an average of 71·6 m.p.h. This was no better than the schedule of the Bristolian demanded but it is heart-warming to think of the Saint quietly dozing at Reading and then leaping into sparkling life to meet the emergency.

A similar happening eighteen years later was recorded in the *Railway Magazine* for January 1955. This time a Castle running the up Bristolian was in trouble with brakes leaking on and was therefore stopped at Little Somerford with the object of sending the news to Swindon, twelve miles further on, as an advance warning of the possible need for another engine. As it happened, a goods train standing on the loop line to allow the Bristolian to pass was headed by a Hall class 2/4–6–0 and this was probably as good a replacement as any that Swindon might be able to produce at short notice. So after due discussion it was decided that the Castle should be replaced there and then by the Hall. Deliberations of this sort take time and the Bristolian started from Little Somerford some 14 minutes after it stopped there. The enginemen hammered No. 7904 *Fountains Hall* as hard as their predecessors had hammered *Clevedon Court* before the war and the result was that speed was worked up to 79 m.p.h. on passing Swindon and the train stopped in Paddington 59 minutes 37 seconds later. Speed was between 80 and 84 m.p.h. for 47 miles between Wantage Road and West Drayton. Here a smaller-wheeled version of the Churchward Saint very markedly beat one of the Great Western's fastest schedules. The rotational speed of the wheels was some 7 per cent higher than that of No. 5006 *Tregenna Castle* in establishing the Swindon-Paddington record of 56 minutes 47 seconds in 1932.

Many examples might be quoted of prolonged hard running of Saints with heavy trains but few are closely comparable with that detailed on p. 193 and described on pp. 145–162.

Collett made four-cylinder engines more than sufficiently numerous to cover all the top-rank Great Western passenger trains and so the Saints were rarely seen in such service after about 1927, but he and his successor built a great many locomotives that were Saints in only very slight disguise.

SIX-FOOT SAINTS,
Hall class (W88) 1928

When one considers the functional difference between a Hall and a Saint one may well ask whether the improvements in the Hall could not have been effected in some less drastic way. By changing the wheel diameter from $80\frac{1}{2}$ in. to 72 in. the speed range for highest cylinder efficiency was dropped in the same ratio of 11 per cent. Instead of 42 to 84 m.p.h. it became 37 to 74 m.p.h. At speeds between 42 and 74 m.p.h. there was nothing to choose between Saint and Hall on the score of useful work obtained from each pound of coal. At speeds below 42 m.p.h., the Hall had some advantage over the Saint, but it was not big enough to be discernible at speeds over about 30 m.p.h.

But whatever the advantage was it could have been obtained with far less fuss, simply by increasing the diameter of the cylinders from $18\frac{1}{2}$ to $19\frac{1}{2}$ in. This would of course increase the maximum piston load due to steam pressure by 11 per cent and it might have been deemed necessary to increase the size of the crank pins on that account. (In settling this point there could have been no better information than that derived from Great Western experience over nearly twenty years with the Saints and the 2–8–0s.)

Assuming that point could have been satisfactorily covered, there was no need for anything but more Saints, stiffened here and there. This last remark arises because the officially-quoted weight of a Hall was 3 tons greater than that of a Saint whereas the only

108

obvious difference – smaller coupled wheels in the Hall – would be expected to make the later engine slightly lighter. So it seems certain that there was in fact greater thickness of metal in certain parts of the Hall.

The advantages of minimizing changes from old standards are not easy to assess and so it is impossible to say whether it would have been better on the whole to have kept to the basic dimensions of the Saint. Equally it is impossible to say that the 6 ft wheel diameter of the Halls had any advantage over the standard 5 ft 8 in. diameter envisaged by Churchward in 1901 and used by Collett in the Granges of 1936.

Be that as it may, the 'six-foot Saints' eventually numbered 330, the last having been built near the end of 1950, forty-seven years after the appearance of No. 98. Churchward had judged well in going ahead with a 2/4-6-0 in 1903 and in designing it so well as to meet needs over fifty years ahead. The only real design-change made by Collett was that he placed the rocking shaft bearings at its ends instead of in the middle.

An epoch-marking change was made by Hawksworth in 1944 by the building of No. 6959 with a plate-frame of the conventional type instead of the plate/bar frame introduced by Churchward in 1903 in order to admit the cylinder/half-saddle construction. The bolted connection between the two frames could work loose over a long life and so could the bolted connections between the strips of the light frame of the Churchward bogie. That also was replaced in No. 6959 by a plate-frame bogie.

The most noticeable feature of these changes was the projection of each frame plate ahead of Holcroft's curved drop plate under the smokebox and the straight slope of the top edge of each plate reminded one of Dean practice.

All Halls after 6959 were built in this way and so were the 1000 class 2/4-6-os introduced in 1945.

FIVE-FOOT-EIGHT SAINTS,
Grange class (W 89) 1936

Whether or not Collett really believed that there was any technical advantage in departing from Churchward standard wheel diameters, he could not escape from using such wheels to replace some 2/2–6–os by 4/4–6–os.

The 6800 class, introduced in 1936 and named as 'Granges' were five-foot-eight Saints incorporating wheels, coupling rods, steps, buffers and so on from 2/2–6–os. One may be sure that financial considerations decided that either existing wheels should be used in the new engines or that there should be no new engines. The anti-standardization boys just had to accept the mortifying fact that from August 1936 to May 1939 Swindon produced eighty locomotives of a design projected by Churchward in 1901 and built entirely of his standard components. Their only little triumph was to get his chimney chopped down by a couple of inches.

With plenty of Halls to cover semi-fast passenger trains and to act as reserves for fully-fast trains only rarely did a Grange get a chance to show what she could do in top-rank passenger-train service. So there is no long list of published logs of running by Granges. But it could well be that they were slightly superior to Saints and Halls on such a route as Shrewsbury to Bristol, where really high speed is prohibited by track curvature.

LIGHT-WEIGHT SAINTS,
Manor class (W90) 1938

Additional power provided for the Cambrian section of the Great Western in 1936 was in the form of double-frame 4–4–os because double frames had become available by scrapping of Bulldog 4–4–os. Obviously Swindon would use these in new engines if it possibly could.

Equally obviously, the ideal engine for the lightly and sinuously laid Cambrian section was a 2/2–6–0. Unfortunately the 4300 class 2/2–6–0 was inadmissibly heavy for this section and moreover some doubts had arisen as to whether the 4300s should be used regularly in fairly fast passenger service on curved lines. Otherwise consideration might well have been given to a smaller-boilered version of the 4300s.

Instead the Saint-style 4–6–0 was taken as the basis of the design of a new class of engine that could be used on weight-restricted routes like the Cambrian, and it was found that the Grange design would do very nicely if the boiler were replaced by an appropriately lighter one. As in the Granges, wheels, steps and so on from scrapped 4300s could be used in what became the Manor class.

A new boiler (No. 14) was designed, in the standard Churchward style but with the novelty, for Swindon, of a slope in the front wall of the firebox between the grate and the underside of the barrel.

Manors were first used to take Newcastle–Swansea trains over the restricted section between Banbury and Cheltenham and it was not until 1943 that they were regularly used on the Cambrian section. Their introduction there, where double-frame 4-4-0s previously ran the passenger trains, was analogous to the appearance forty years earlier of 2/4-6-0s on the London–Bristol route where Atbara and City double-frame 4-4-0s were in common use.

HIGH-PRESSURE 'SAINTS'
1000 class 2/4-6-0 (W91) 1945 later named after Counties

The 1000 class 2/4-6-0 was a pathetic design and this was largely because it was produced for no real reason. Since 1903 high boiler pressure had been a Great Western speciality and so when in 1941 the first Southern Railway Pacific was announced to have a boiler pressure (280 p.s.i.) 30 p.s.i. higher than any other in Britain, Swindon felt this to be a deliberate challenge or gibe. It was intolerable that the Great Western should have ceased to be Britain's leader in this field and so means were sought to correct the situation as soon as might be by building a Great Western engine with steam at 280 p.s.i. Nothing of this kind could be done while World War II was still raging (some very forceful comments had been made about the loss of war effort associated with the production of the Southern Pacifics) and there would be plenty of bread-and-butter work to be done for quite a time after it ended, but at least Swindon could think about it.

The first essential was to give the locomotive driving wheels big enough for express-passenger-train services but to describe it as a mixed-traffic locomotive, in order to counter in advance any suggestion that it was not well-suited to goods traffic. This artifice had sufficed for Bulleid to secure for the Southern Railway permission to introduce a new design of Pacific in wartime. To reinforce this in trying to get post-war permission from the authorities, Swindon used in *its* design of a 280-pounder the boiler of the LMS Class 8F 2–8–os, indisputably a goods-engine boiler.

A preliminary announcement suggested that the new engine was being built primarily for service in Cornwall. Its dimensions were consistent with this inasmuch as it was (on paper) a two-cylinder equivalent of a Castle that did not need to be a flyer. An easier solution to the design problem was simply to mount a Castle boiler on the chassis of a Hall, with appropriately-enlarged cylinders. This would not have been noticeably novel and no one at Swindon would have been happy with cylinders bigger than those used by Churchward.

The need for larger cylinders was avoided by matching the Southern's 280 p.s.i. and the use of the 8F boiler announced that Swindon was not rigidly tied to Churchward designs, although in all conscience little in the 8F boiler suggested any other origin.

Continuous splashers announced that both Churchward and Collett had been superseded, and another new look came from a redesigned tender that was fractionally lighter than the current standard one.

The cab was widened by a few inches in a manner that left no foothold outside it and this deprived enginemen of the normal escape route from dangerous conditions on the footplate. When steam and fire were flying about in the cab, it was vital to be able to get ahead of it all, but they would have to find their own way of reaching safety from the cab of the 280 p.s.i. 1000 class.

This final form of the Saint appeared some forty years after its origin. The only real difference, apart from a small increase in the size of the boiler, was that the cab gave more shelter when running normally but made certain types of accident more dangerous for the crew.

No. 1000 herself was built with a double chimney that looked grossly out of proportion to the rest of the locomotive but the other members of the class came out with standard single chimneys and they looked quite respectable.

There was nothing in the dimensions or style of the 1000 class to suggest that it could be more effective than a Castle and no published record of work by a 1000 inclined one to any more generous assessment of their capabilities.

When at length the Southern had tired of the 280 p.s.i. frolic and reduced the boiler pressure of the Bulleid Pacifics to 250 p.s.i., the Great Western did the same with the 1000s.

The only obvious departures in the design of the 1000s from Churchward precepts were the use of full-length plate frames (as in the 6959 class), of plate-frame bogies and of a continuous splasher over the coupled wheels on each side of the engine. This last departure had previously been made in a Castle and a King when they were semi-streamlined in 1935. Some people liked the look of it; some were not so sure.

The really epoch-marking departure of No. 1000 from established Swindon practice was the use of a 'hopper-type' ashpan. This means that the ashpan was shaped so that most of the accumulated ash would slide down out of it when a door in the bottom of it was opened. It is a severe criticism of British locomotive design practice in general that such devices had hardly ever been used in Britain until the later stages of World War II.

American-built 2/2–8–0s, brought into Britain in readiness to go to Europe as soon as a landing had been effected, were used on goods trains on British railways and showed railway staff how much unpleasant labour could be avoided by use of hopper-type ashpans. There was nothing novel in the principle as it had been tried in England nearly a century earlier. Only its apparent importation from abroad persuaded our locomotive engineers that it might warrant extensive and prolonged trial.

Dumping char and ash into a pit between the rails is not much use unless the pit can be emptied completely, readily and easily. At very few British sheds was this the case and this may explain why the hopper-type ashpan was not widely used on British locomotives.

In later years some of the 2/4–6–0 Counties were given double chimneys of which the top was distinctly lower than the top of the safety-valve casing and the cab roof. So far as draughting is concerned, the chimney may be as tall as the loading gauge permits and it was usual to take advantage of this freedom in design. In the Counties this was not done and it cannot be claimed that a taller chimney would have been less effective.

The probability is that the short double chimney was adopted simply because a tall one dominates the whole aspect of the loco- motive and this had been painfully obvious in No. 1000. So although the disparity in height between the chimney and the safety valve looked rather odd, this was preferable to the alternative of a tall double chimney that made the engine itself look trivial.

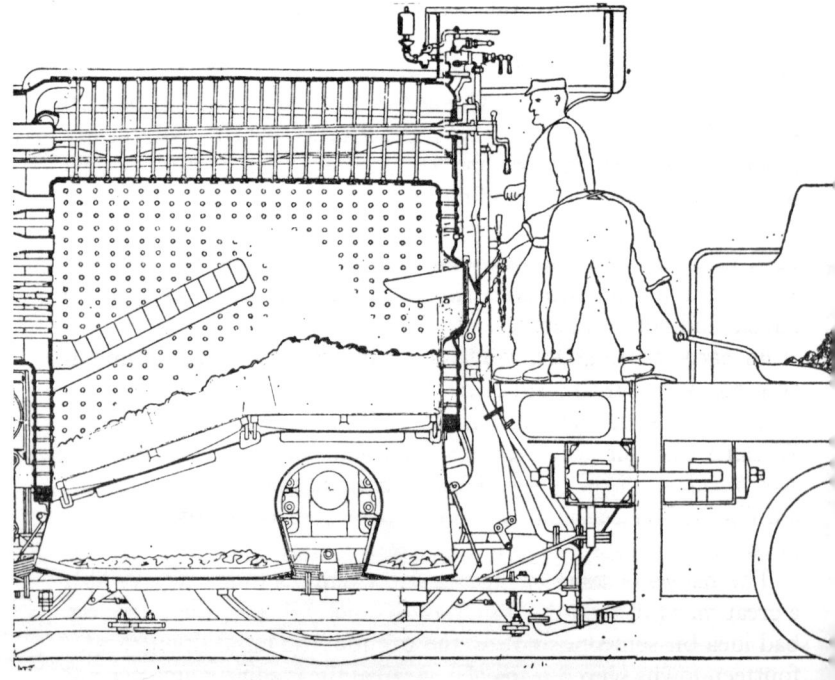

Fig. VII. At work on a Saint with a hot fire.

CHAPTER 7

Naming of Locomotives

Draught-horses were usually given names, and so it was natural for the early steam locomotives to have them too, as they were the mechanical equivalents of draught-horses. Moreover, when engineers were feeling their way in the early days of development, every new locomotive tended to be different from its predecessors and had such high hopes associated with it as to justify a rather more emotional identification than a mere number. When a design had so well established itself as to justify production in quantity, the need arose for means of distinction between the physically identical members of a class and for that purpose numbers might well seem more natural than names.

Most railways in Britain soon got round to numbering their loco-motives even though they had named them as well. On the Great Western Railway, however, the 419 broad-gauge engines were named and not numbered.

As early as 1837 the principle had been applied of using a common word in the names of all the locomotives of a class as a means of causing the name to identify the class. The first Great Western example was the Star class with twelve names such as *North Star* and *Royal Star*. Eleven of the names were used again for a different Star class introduced in 1907; four of the names could be identified with Venus and three with Stella Polaris.

The names of broad-gauge engines were very varied, although a great many of them had an obvious classical background. A very bad idea bit someone in 1865 and eventually caused the names of fourteen towns served by the Great Western Railway to be given to locomotives. It may well have been deemed incredible that any passenger would imagine the name of a town on a locomotive to be a destination indicator, but it did happen, perhaps not very frequently, and it was not until 1927 that any Great Western locomotive was renamed specifically to avoid any risk that a traveller might be misled.

A fair proportion of Great Western standard-gauge engines had names besides numbers. Personalities and places associated with the Boer War provided inspiration for some names given in 1900. Other names may have come from battleships or the like and this seems to be the origin of two Atbara names *Powerful* and *Terrible*, but the second of these has lost what powerful impression it may originally have made because a common meaning is now the one conveyed by a heavily defeated American boxer when he said, 'Gee! I was terrible.' (*Atbara* itself is an Egyptian river-name attached to a Kitchener victory (1898) on its northern bank near Nakheila.)

The naming of the last twenty Atbaras after flowers is said to be associated with Churchward's active interest in gardening and the naming of the last twenty Bulldogs after birds may have some connection with his addiction to shooting.

But the naming of the 2/4-6-os Nos 2901 to 2910 as Ladies was an inspiration. It may be added that the much later Great Western locomotive *Lady Margaret Hall* was neither a Lady nor a Saint but a Hall, just as *Duke of York, Duke of Edinburgh, Duke of Connaught* and *Duke of Cambridge* were not Dukes.

There are widely different opinions on the value and propriety of applying names to locomotives, and there are divided opinions on the choice of names. The principle that arrives at *Swallow*, to hint at speed, or *Tornado*, to suggest energy, is hampered by lack of sufficient names for application to hundreds of locomotives. The class-name principle which has (perhaps) some practical value was applied on the Great Western to hundreds of Castles, Halls, Granges and Manors and some commentators object to the monotony of the recurrence of the class name in the full list of names. This, however, has no bearing on the question as to whether a Castle name or Hall name is appropriate for a particular locomotive. What seems to the writer to be important is that the name should not be ugly or undignified. Among the very few Great Western transgressions may be mentioned *Dummer Grange* which is ugly, *Marble Hall* which is slightly flippant, and *Coity Castle* which saucily suggests an establishment not primarily devoted to defence.

Judged by the names of its locomotives the Great Western was strongly inclined to be 'county'. Besides actual Counties it had Dukes, Earls, hundreds of stately homes prinked with Flowers and Birds. This fits in well with one's impression of the Great Western locomotives speeding through rich rolling parkland to the golden west.

The very numerous names of London & North Western locomotives had such extraordinary variety as to give no strong impression of any particular character.

The engine names that became common on the East-Coast route out of London were in themselves delightfully varied, but one could not forget their association with race meetings. The place-names given to engines on the Great Eastern section of the LNER could, with some research, be associated with stately homes, but the other names were emphatically those of football teams.

The LMS engine names were largely associated with warfare and British possessions.

With this background of comparison, one feels that criticism of Great Western naming policy cannot be more than trivial. Superiority may perhaps be claimed for Southern Railway King Arthur names associated with faerie lands now alas, forlorn of railways.

Selection of a name for a locomotive is a subject for careful thought and no less so is the method of its display on the locomotive. Swindon did quite a lot of experimenting with alternatives in the period from 1898 to 1903. Some of these were strange or ugly but the finally-selected style, which persisted on nearly all of the hundreds of named engines ever afterwards built at Swindon, was magnificent. Superbly formed letters proudly spread in a majestic arc on a brass-edged plate surpassed all that had been used before and all that other railways used afterwards.

'Why did the Great Western have wider popularity than the other railways?' people continue to ask. Apart from the obvious answer, 'Because it was the best', one may suggest that its locomotive-naming policy was a major factor. The man-on-the-platform may be impressed by a locomotive without knowing much about it as a machine, but he could read and remember a name, and especially if it were displayed in dignified splendour.

The names applied to the Churchward 2/4-6-0s were for the most part strikingly different in character from those of contemporary locomotives on other railways, and they make an interesting study.

The name 'Saints' was often applied to the 77 Churchward 2/4-6-0s although only twenty of them carried saint names.

NUMBERS AND NAMES (AND THEIR ORIGINS)
OF THE 2900S

| 2900 *William Dean* | Locomotive superintendent |

THE LADIES

2901 *Lady Superior*	Lady superintendent
2902 *Lady of the Lake*	Title of Scott novel
2903 *Lady of Lyons*	Title of comedy by Bulwer-Lytton
2904 *Lady Godiva*	Nude horse-rider of Coventry
2905 *Lady Macbeth*	Shakespearean character
2906 *Lady of Lynn*	Title of novel by Sir Walter Besant
2907 *Lady Disdain*	*Much Ado About Nothing*, I, i (121)
2908 *Lady of Quality*	Title of novel by Frances Hodgson Burnett
2909 *Lady of Provence*	Title of novel by Charlotte M. Tucker
2910 *Lady of Shalott*	Tennyson character

THE SAINTS

2911 *Saint Agatha*	Virgin martyr of Catonia in Sicily in third century. Feast day February 5th. Died from prolonged tortures.
2912 *Saint Ambrose*	Bishop and doctor, AD 334-397. Feast day December 7th. Was Bishop of Milan, from 374 BC, when it was the administrative centre of the western part of the Roman empire. Developed the singing of hymns as a popular means of divine praise.
2913 *Saint Andrew*	Apostle. Galilean fisherman of Bethsaida. Feast day November 30th. Patron saint of Scotland.
2914 *Saint Augustine*	Bishop and doctor, AD 354-430. Feast day August 28th. Born in Thagaste (Algeria). Great writer. For thirty-four years was

		Bishop of Hippo (North Africa). One of the most distinguished bishops in the history of Christianity.
2915	*Saint Bartholomew*	Apostle. Feast day August 24th. No other reliable history.
2916	*Saint Benedict.*	Patriarch of Western monks, AD 480–547. Feast day March 21st. His insistence on discipline was not liked by everyone.
2917	*Saint Bernard*	Abbot and theologian, AD 1090–1153. Great organizer and prolific writer.
2918	*Saint Catherine*	Legendary figure associated with Alexandria. Feast day November 25th. (There are at least six authenticated Saint Catherines, or Katherines, dating from 1303.)
2919	*Saint Cuthbert*	Bishop, AD 634–687. Feast day March 20th. Northumbrian naturalist. Travelled constantly to minister to the scattered peoples of the border-country and Galloway. Had a retreat on Farne Island where he died.
2920	*Saint David*	Abbot-bishop. Sixth century. Feast day March 1st. Patron saint of Wales. Founded several monasteries in Wales.
2921	*Saint Dunstan*	Bishop AD 909–988. Feast day May 19th. At Glastonbury in 943 started the revival of organized monasticism in England. Archbishop of Canterbury from 959. Singer, musician, metal-worker.
2922	*Saint Gabriel*	Archangel. Feast day September 29th.
2923	*Saint George*	Martyr, third-fourth century. Feast day April 23rd. Patron saint of England.
2924	*Saint Helena*	Empress, AD 255–330. Feast day August 18th. Mother of Constantine the Great. Name associated with the rediscovery of the Cross of Christ in the fourth century.
2925	*Saint Martin*	Pope and martyr, AD d.655. Feast day November. Elected Pope, AD 649. Died from ill-treatment directed by Byzantine emperor Constans II.
2926	*Saint Nicholas*	Bishop. Fourth century. Feast day December. Bishop of Myra in Lycia (south-western Asia Minor). No other reliable history. Patron saint of children and many other things.
2927	*Saint Patrick*	Missionary bishop, AD 385–461. Feast day March 17th. Evangelizer of the Irish. Patron saint of Ireland.

2928	*Saint Sebastian.*	Martyr. Date unknown. Feast day January 20th. Murdered under the direction of Diocletian. Buried near the Appian Way at Rome. Favourite subject for Renaissance painters.	
2929	*Saint Stephen*	First Christian martyr, Jerusalem, about AD 35. Feast day December 26th. Probably a Greek-speaking Jew. A zealous preacher who arraigned the Jewish council and was stoned to death by its direction.	
2930	*Saint Vincent*	Martyr. Feast day January 22. Killed in Valencia (Spain) in AD 304 in the persecution directed by Diocletian.	

THE COURTS

2931	*Arlington Court*	5 miles NNE.	of Barnstaple
2932	*Ashton Court*	3 miles WSW.	of Bristol
2933	*Bibury Court*	9 miles NE.	of Cirencester
2934	*Butleigh Court*	4 miles ESE.	of Glastonbury
2935	*Caynham Court*	3 miles SE.	of Ludlow
2936	*Cefntilla Court*	10 miles SSE.	of Abergavenny
2937	*Clevedon Court*	10 miles WSW.	of Bristol
2938	*Corsham Court*	4 miles SW	of Chippenham
2939	*Croome Court*	8 miles E.	of Great Malvern
2940	*Dorney Court*	3 miles W.	of Slough
2941	*Easton Court*	5 miles SSE.	of Ludlow
2942	*Fawley Court*	1 mile N.	of Henley-on-Thames
2943	*Hampton Court*	1 mile SW.	of Kingston-on-Thames
2944	*Highnam Court*	3 miles WNW.	of Gloucester
2945	*Hillingdon Court*	1 mile E.	of Uxbridge
2946	*Langford Court*	11 miles SW.	of Bristol
2947	*Madresfield Court*	3 miles ENE.	of Great Malvern
2948	*Stackpole Court*	3 miles S.	of Pembroke
2949	*Stanford Court*	10 miles SW.	of Kidderminster
2950	*Taplow Court*	2 miles E.	of Maidenhead
2951	*Tawstock Court*	2 miles S.	of Barnstaple
2952	*Twineham Court*	10 miles NNW.	of Brighton
2953	*Titley Court*	9 miles W.	of Leominster
2954	*Tockenham Court*	9 miles WSW.	of Swindon
2955	*Tortworth Court*	14 miles NNE.	of Bristol

OTHERS

2971	*Albion*	To match *La France*
2972	*The Abbot*	Scott novel

2973	*Robins Bolitho*	Director
2974	*Lord Barrymore*	Director
2975	*Sir Ernest Palmer*	Director
2976	*Winterstoke*	Director
2972	*Robertson*	Director
2978	*Kirkland*	Director
2979	*Quentin Durward*	Scott novel
2980	*Coeur de Lion*	King Richard
2981	*Ivanhoe*	Scott novel
2982	*Lalla Rookh*	Title of poem by Thomas More 1771–1852
2983	*Redgauntlet*	Scott novel
2984	*Guy Mannering*	Scott novel
2985	*Peveril of the Peak*	Scott novel
2986	*Robin Hood*	Scott novel
2987	*Bride of Lammermoor*	Scott novel
2988	*Rob Roy*	Scott novel
2989	*Talisman*	Scott novel
2990	*Waverley*	Scott novel
2998	*Ernest Cunard*	Director

No. 2998 was originally No. 98. Every other number above 2955 was greater by 2800 than the original number of the engine.

No. 2972 and Nos. 2979 to 2990 were 2/4–4–2s before becoming 2/4–6–0s.

The word 'Saint' or the contraction 'St' appeared in the names of certain Great Western locomotives that were not of the Saint class. In the following list are given the numbers carried by such locomotives before and after the renumbering in 1913.

SOME GREAT WESTERN LOCOMOTIVES THAT WERE NOT 'SAINTS'

		Class	
Saint Bride's Hall	4972	Hall	(W88)
Saint Benet's Hall	5947	Hall	(W88)
Saint Edmund Hall	5960	Hall	(W88)
Saint Peter's Hall	7900	Hall	(W88)
St Agnes	3287/3276	Duke	(W35)
St Anthony	3264/3303	Duke	(W35)
St Aubyn	3367/3355	Bulldog	(W42)
St Austell	3326/3289	Duke	(W35)
St Columb	3325/3316	Duke	(W35)
St Donat's Castle	5017	Castle	(W86)
St Erth	3285/3275	Duke	(W35)

St Fagan's Castle	5067	Castle	(W86)
St George	3025	3001	(W27)
St Germans	3265/3261	Duke	(W35)
St Johns	3411/4147	Atbara	(W43)
St Just	3286/3310	Duke	(W35)
St Mawes Castle	5018	Castle	(W86)
St Michael	3267/3263	Duke	(W35)

CHAPTER 8

Speed and Performance

Round about May 1848 a Great Western locomotive and train ran from Paddington to Didcot, about 53 miles, against a slight gradient in about 48 minutes. Someone was sufficiently impressed to prepare a commemorative card that quoted

Broad-gauge engine *Great Britain*
9.15 Express to Bristol
Four carriages and van
Paddington to Didcot   53¼ miles
Time (start-to-stop)   47 minutes
Date   11 May 1848

The fact of specially printing these details no doubt convinced some people that they were authentic. MacDermot, however, in his *History of the Great Western Railway*, refers to the story as 'a long-standing Great Western tradition' and this suggests that he did not believe it. Justification for his doubt was shown in an article contributed to the *Railway Magazine* for March 1939 by Canon Reginald B. Fellows, who remarked:

' (a) in 1848 there was no train leaving Paddington at 9.15 for Bristol or Didcot:

(b) the distance of 53¼ miles is the mileage from the new Paddington station which was not opened till 1854.'

He also recorded that on May 10, 1848, there was a bad accident that killed six passengers and injured thirteen others at Shrivenham. So it was most improbable that any 'speeding' would be attempted on the following morning.

If one accepts his remarks, the card was incorrect in the starting time of the train and in the statement of distance run; inevitably doubt arises in connection with the time of 47 minutes.

The matter was pursued by correspondents in the *Railway Magazine* for May 1939 and for February 1940 but, perhaps unavoidably in connection with something that happened over ninety years earlier, nothing clear-cut was established.

In 1848 Gooch presented a paper on the subject of train resistance and referred to an express that 'was in the constant practice of running the 53 miles to Didcot, without stopping, in 48 to 50 minutes'.

It may perhaps be concluded that on one occasion at least the 53 miles were covered in about 49 minutes at a start-to-stop average of 65 m.p.h. This was sufficiently notable in 1848 and indeed over eighty years had to elapse before any Great Western train (or any other in Britain) was publicly scheduled to run regularly at such a speed.

Authentic or not, the 1848 episode established a speed-reputation that lasted over many years during which Great Western trains were not notably fast. From 1902, however, sustained fast running by Churchward locomotives re-established the Great Western in the speed realm and for the next thirty years or so it could be claimed to be the fastest line in Britain.

HIGHEST SPEEDS

Although the commercially useful speed of a railway was the average speed regularly achieved by its publicly time-tabled trains in running from important place A to important place B, whenever that average was much higher than any other means of transport could offer it was always interesting to know what was the highest speed attained, even for a few seconds, by any train.

Naturally one expects top speed to be reached downhill and at the bottom of a downhill where the line is not sharply curved and where there is plenty of 'run-out' in which to slow down to any speed restriction ahead.

On looking over the gradient profiles of the Great Western Railway and thinking of the curvature one finds that incomparably the best place is the Severn Tunnel. Going west from Patchway are

7 miles averaging 1 in 115 down with no speed restriction, the last 3 miles being uniformly at 1 in 100. Then after a short level stretch there are 3 miles *up* at 1 in 90 so that even quite light braking would suffice to stop the train at the next stop signal at Severn Tunnel West Box.

Anyone who thought of this in the years immediately following the opening of the tunnel in 1885 might be put off by the thought that it was impossible to measure the speed of the train because no timing points could be seen in the darkness of the tunnel. And anyway would it be sensible for any driver to go very fast in a tunnel, and especially a tunnel under water? As against that, he might reflect that about half the drivers who worked regularly through the tunnel were Welshmen and moreover from South Wales. When running westwards they would be going home and if they thought it was impossible for anyone to time the train at its fastest why need they worry about letting her go?

In the 1880s speeds between 80 and 85 m.p.h. had been noted down the bank from Whiteball to Wellington (Somerset), on coming out of the bottom end of Box Tunnel, and in going down from Chipping Campden to Honeybourne on the way to Worcester, all on gradients of about 1 in 100, but there seems to be nothing on record of what was done on the real speed-way under the Severn. Not until September 1938 did any published record suggest that a train had touched 100 m.p.h. at the bottom of the Severn Tunnel. No other published record suggests any speed quite so high as this but the (probable) rarity with which maximum speeds were ever measured in this vicinity makes it improbable that the observed 98 m.p.h. was the highest ever. It was achieved by Castle No. 5052 in the course of an otherwise undistinguished run of the 1.55 p.m. train from Paddington to Newport; it was of 13 coaches grossing 420 tons.

The first reasonably well-authenticated speed of 100 m.p.h. on the GW was that made by double-frame 4–4–0 No. 3440 *City of Truro* during a reckless record-breaking run from Plymouth to Bristol on 9 May 1904. The adjective 'reckless' is included because the train ran down the helter-skelter from Brent to Totnes in South Devon at an average of 69·6 m.p.h. with a maximum of 77 and down the corkscrew from Dainton to Aller Junction and on to

Newton Abbot at 57·6 m.p.h. average. But even this driver had his limit. Down the serpentine stretch from Whiteball to Wellington he got up to about 100 m.p.h. and then his nerve failed. Platelayers working on the line ahead provided a timely excuse for braking hard at a point where continuance of full regulator opening might have pushed speed up towards 110 m.p.h. if the train had remained on the rails. But the driver evidently had doubts about this. No published record shows any other train ever to have reached 100 m.p.h. in this vicinity.

The next incident to be recorded in this series was one of the most extraordinary happenings ever admitted by a responsible official of a British railway. It is important in that it enables one to say with reasonable certainty that the highest speed by steam on the Great Western Railway was attained by two-cylinder 4-6-0 No. 2903 in May 1906. The figure quoted was 120 m.p.h. and this was confirmed in a very rough way by the recorded passing times at two signal boxes; these worked out at about 135 m.p.h.

It was regular practice to give engines newly-built at Swindon a running-in trip from there to Stoke Gifford and back, a total distance of about 70 miles. This test-track was used instead of the Paddington–Bristol main line because there was less traffic on it and because the triangle of lines at Stoke Gifford was a convenient means of turning engines for the return journey to Swindon. It includes a straight descent of 9 miles at 1 in 300 to Little Somerford, followed by a rise of 6 miles at 1 in 300 leaving plenty of room for stopping. It was usual for every engine that behaved normally on the outward journey to be run pretty fast on the way back.

So far so good, but the 1906 incident started a rumour of 'two miles a minute' and this became so persistent a legend that eventually someone persuaded Mr C. B. Collett to admit that a group of 'high-ups' at Swindon had indulged in a bit of horseplay. The *Railway Magazine* for April 1932 states on p. 305 that, on the evidence of Mr Collett,

'The purpose of the run was to demonstrate that an engine taken straight from the shops could be run at over 100 miles per hour. Those on the footplate included Mr Collett, who was then

Assistant Manager of the Locomotive Works, Mr G. H. Flewellen, who was Locomotive Inspector, and the Foreman of the Erecting Shop, Mr Evans. (The driver was Mr H. J. Robinson.) The timing for some distance by the mileposts with a stop-watch was given as 120 miles per hour, and the clocking between the signal-boxes of Little Somerford and Hullavington was booked as two minutes for the $4\frac{1}{2}$ miles.

'Mr Collett points out that, while the object of running a new engine on its first trip at over 100 miles per hour was achieved, the timing could not be regarded as accurate and that the 102·3 m.p.h. record of the *City of Truro* in 1904, made under the personal observation of one of the most careful recorders of his time – the late Charles Rous-Marten – with the aid of a chronograph reading to one-fifth parts of a second, must remain the best duly authenticated railway speed record that this country has yet witnessed.'

As GW engines at that time were never required to exceed 90 m.p.h. in ordinary service and were put on fast jobs only after running for a week or two on slow ones, there was no technical need to know whether a newly built engine could reach 100 m.p.h. So why was it desired to know it? Had anyone worked out at what speed the balance weights of a Lady would lift her driving wheels off the rails in every revolution?

They wanted to know whether the Lady could run at over 100 m.p.h. on her maiden excursion. But if that was all, why go up to 120 m.p.h. where out-of-balance forces were nearly half as big again? Had they developed a kind of mob-hysteria that led them to urge the driver to go 'all out' regardless of everything? By the time they had run more sedately on to Swindon and the disciplined serenity of the Works they probably agreed that not a word of this sporting venture should be whispered to anyone. No intention of this kind is ever more than a pious hope and every student of the steam locomotive must be glad that an official statement was eventually made.

It was most imprudent to allow so many officials to participate in what was undoubtedly a risky exploit, and these sporty souls would naturally pick a day when Churchward was away from Swindon.

Had he gained any hint of such intention he would have forbidden it for one obvious reason in some such terms, as 'If you go and get yourselves all killed, where the bloody hell am I?'

What really did happen on this extraordinary occasion? No one concerned would say a word while the incident was fresh in any-one's mind although it was admitted that a speed of about two miles a minute was reached. One is justified in resorting to conjecture and the fact that the engine had pole reversing gear, which is not safely adjustable at speed, makes one wonder whether this was a factor.

It is possible that the driver had found that his original pole-setting was not producing 100 m.p.h., and was thereupon persuaded by one of the officials to try a little later cut-off. If he were rash enough to attempt this (or if someone else said 'Here, let me do it') the engine might well drop into full gear and accelerate like mad. Everyone might then be so appalled by the exhaust noise of such running as to do nothing at first to neutralize it, until by the time the driver had recovered from the shock of having the pole pulled out of his hand and had got round to turning the blower on and shutting the regulator, some unabashed spirit said, 'No! leave her at that. Let's see what she'll do.'

Or did the driver try to close the regulator and find that he couldn't? A big flow of steam from the boiler will sometimes cause such a pressure drop from one side of the regulator-valve to the other that the valve becomes very hard to move and if an engine without a train is running very fast downhill with steam urging it on, its brakes won't stop it quickly, if at all.

If anything of this sort happened on *Lady of Lyons*, already doing nearly 100 m.p.h. down 1 in 300, there could have been plenty of lively apprehension on the footplate. With driving wheels leaving the rails eight times per second, with the engine using water so fast that the fusible plugs were at risk and with the impossibility of stopping in any distance less than about six miles, someone had to do something. There were plenty of people there, and so two could pull at the reversing pole and two at the regulator handle while someone else made sure that both injectors were working and then, still remembering what they had come for, took some mile-post-passing times.

ba. No. 891 2/4–6–0 Atchinson, Topeka and Santa Fe RR (p. 79).

No. 3826 (W110) *County of Flint,* Churchward County.

No. 181 (W107) *Ivanhoe.* Later converted to 2/4–6–0 (W84).

No. 2990 (W84) *Waverley.* Originally an Atlantic, No. 190, like No. 181 above.

11a. No. 2925 (W88) *Saint Martin*. Converted from (W84) in 1924.

b. No. 4915 (W88) *Condover Hall* as later fitted with outside steam pipes to cylinders.

c. No. 6825 (W89) *Llanvair Grange*. Wheels and tender from scrapped 2/2–6–0 (W96).

d. No. 7803 (W90) *Barcote Manor*.

Evidently they did get things under control at last, with 100 m.p.h. well and truly exceeded and everybody on board still shaking. The sensible ones would realize that they'd only had what they'd asked for and had been lucky to get away with it. After the white faces there would be metaphorical red ones, and no desire to admit to anyone what danger they had produced for themselves and the engine.

This is only a guess. What a pity that they didn't have anything like the black box that aircraft now carry to take a record of what went on during alarming last moments! The nearest equivalent to it was provided by the signalmen at Hullavington and Little Somerford. Their evidence of roughly 135 m.p.h. tended to show that Collett's report of about 120 m.p.h. was not an exaggerated one but he himself admitted it and disclaimed it in the same sentence. An interpretation of this is that the speed was attained but in circumstances that did not do much credit to those responsible for the exploit.

The next known G W '100' was achieved in 1939 by No. 4086 *Builth Castle* at the head of a 255-ton train when passing Honeybourne after running 4½ miles down at 1 in 100. The 100 m.p.h. could be run without overloading the track as a four-cylinder engine can be balanced so that its hammer blow is very much less than that of a two-cylinder engine of comparable size.

After World War II and a long recovery period the daily down-and-up Bristolian was brought back to pre-war timing and the highest daily speeds on the Great Western were attained at Dauntsey on the way down from Swindon to Chippenham and at Little Somerford where *Lady of Lyons* had done her stuff. Maxima of over 90 m.p.h. became not uncommon at these points, and 100 m.p.h. was occasionally approached.

An incredible rumour arose that a King had touched 110 m.p.h. at Curry Rivell down on the Athelney marshes on the way from Westbury to Taunton. The actual figure turned out to be 100 m.p.h and this was sufficiently remarkable in that vicinity. The same comment applies to a maximum of 103 m.p.h. reached by a King at Lavington on the way down from Savernake to Westbury.

LOCOMOTIVE PERFORMANCE

A locomotive's job is to pull a train from A to B in a specified time and a child who rides on the train and looks twice at an ordinary watch can see whether it has done that job or not. An interested boy might amplify observation of this character by making notes of the passing times of the train at intermediate stations and signal-boxes. If he had a watch with a seconds hand and knew the lengths of the rails he might ascertain average speeds over short distances and so be able to determine maximum and minimum speeds in any vicinity. This is all so easy that, among railway enthusiasts, train-timing became such a popular pastime that amateurs have among them far more detailed information about the running of passenger trains on British railways than have the responsible officials.

It is easy to slip into the error of regarding this kind of information about the running of any particular class of locomotive as representing its performance whereas it is in fact only one aspect of it. It is of course the most important aspect in the eyes of the public and of the Traffic Department of the railway and it may be held that if a locomotive cannot 'keep time' no virtue it may have can cancel this deficiency, but in the full life of the locomotive quite different things also matter. It is perhaps remarkable, and certainly unfortunate, that none of those other things can be numerically assessed by anybody with anything like the precision that a child with an ordinary watch can bring to bear on time-keeping on any particular train. The amateur can be excused for failing to realize that figures for locomotive performance in general have far wider ranges of uncertainty than those associated with the figures recorded by train-timing enthusiasts.

Such an enthusiast may appreciate a particular performance for any one (or more) of several reasons. He may note, for example, that a particular train started punctually, reached each publicly-booked stop a few seconds before the scheduled time and was a few seconds early at each of the intermediate places for which the working time-table specified a time. This showed that the locomotive was on top of the job but more particularly that the driver had sufficient interest and skill to run the train in line with the book and without any unnecessarily fast or hard running.

But what most enthusiasts preferred was a run during which the engine was worked much harder than the schedule demanded for such good reason as to neutralize loss of time by delays or for a less good reason, such as that the enginemen felt like it. Few enthusiasts could fail to be thrilled when some engine was worked hard, fast, and noisily in beating scheduled times with a train much heavier than usual. Collection of information about occasions of this sort inevitably led to comparisons between the abilities of different classes of locomotive to develop higher power in relation to size and thus to be able to bring late-running heavy trains back on to schedule.

Extensive study of this subject led to the conclusion that a fair measure of the ability of a locomotive to develop high power for its size was sustained drawbar horsepower per sq. ft of grate area. It was quite clear that the length of time for which the power was sustained was an important factor (absolute hell can be knocked out of an engine for a minute or two without impairing its ability to carry on) and this had to be taken into account. A rational basis was established for grading hot performances of hand-fired locomotives of all railways.

On this basis Grade 20 represents a high-class standard that many classes of locomotive were not known ever to have attained. Great Western 4–6–0s had produced performances in Grades 21, 22 and 23. The only British locomotive to surpass this was a double-chimney Gresley A4 Pacific hauling 730 tons on the LNER between Darlington and York with a performance in Grade 26.

More recently the details on p. 193 have been assembled on the basis of figures recorded by the late Mr E. K. Harrison and these show a Great Western Saint in Grade 25. The recorder went to the unusual length of taking some observations of coal consumption and although nothing very precise can be deduced from them it is certain that on this remarkable journey the coal consumption was high in relation to the work done. This is inevitably the case where a locomotive is being worked very hard and it is a perfectly valid reason why an engine driver should not attempt to recover lost time by thrashing the engine.

On the run of No. 2922 some 900 shovelfuls of coal were fed

into the firebox between London and Plymouth. The coal consumption was probably greater than that as it is usual to finish a run with less fire on the grate than there was at the start. On the other hand, little coal would be consumed between Wrangaton and Plymouth and it would not have been sensible to try to climb the bank from Totnes to Wrangaton with a very thin fire. So perhaps the difference between initial and final depths of fire may be ignored.

The crucial questions are, 'How much coal is there in a shovelful?' and 'How many shovel-shots were of shovelfuls?' The Great Western standard firing shovel was much larger than those common on other British railways and could hold 20 lb. of coal. A common assessment of a shovelful was 10 lb. Tentatively adopting the mean figure of 15 lb., the total consumption was about 13,500 lb. or 60 lb. per mile. This may be compared with 47 lb. per mile by No. 4074 *Caldicot Castle* on May 2, 1925 when similar times were achieved with loads not quite so great as those taken by *Saint Gabriel*. This excess of 27 per cent by the smaller engine is no more than might be expected. It is indeed possible that the average shovelful was nearer 20 lb. than 15 and that even 70 lb. were burned per mile. This would amount to a total of 7 tons which exceeds the 'official' figure of 6 tons for the coal capacity of the tender. That figure was very conservative as 7 tons could be taken without rising above the coping plates and a modest heap above that level could add 2 more tons.

Some idea of the human effort required may be gained from the reflection that the driver and fireman between them averaged four shovelfuls per minute for $3\frac{1}{2}$ hours. No wonder that enginemen on the 'Limited' were often 'glad to see Brent'. No wonder that lineside watchers rarely saw anything like gaiety on the footplate as the engine of the 'Limited' blasted up to Dainton tunnel. With recollection of such conditions in mind, the student of locomotive performance may fail to find inspiration in the operation of London–Plymouth trains by diesel locomotives each in charge of one man doing very little and another doing nothing. It was perhaps to be expected that men on such unexciting jobs were apt to fall asleep – the two men on one locomotive at times – and the results could be multiply fatal.

CHAPTER 9

Possible Developments

KING-SIZE SAINT

Churchward could (and did) sketch out a super-Saint simply by applying the No. 7 Standard boiler to the standard Saint chassis (see p. 100). The length of the barrel of that boiler was the same (14 ft 10 in.) as that of the No. 1 boiler but the firebox was a foot longer. As that extra foot could be allowed to push back into the cab (the enginemen wouldn't mind much) the big boiler could be got in without any real trouble and so there you had a 110 per cent Saint. There might well be objection from the Civil Engineer about the extra weight on the 27 ft 9 in. wheelbase and that thought did in fact prohibit production of a Star with a No. 7 boiler. That is why the Castle of 1923 had a new boiler bigger than the No. 1 but smaller than the No. 7.

When in 1927 the General Manager instructed the Civil Engineer to state specifically the position about allowable axle loads, it was found that the No. 7 boiler could in fact have been used on the Star wheelbase to produce a bigger engine than the Castle. An ancient tiff between Churchward and Grierson (Chief Civil Engineer 1904 to 1923) had prohibited proper intercourse between their departments and so in designing the Castle Collett had imposed on himself a weight restriction that was by then out of date.

So the Super-Saint visualized by Churchward might also have been practicable in 1922. This is not certain, however, even though a Super-Star with a No. 7 boiler could have been accepted, because the two-cylinder engine adds substantial hammer blow to its nominal axle loading. But ignoring any possibility of a Super-Saint in 1922, it is interesting to consider such an engine in 1927 when 22½-ton axle-loading was permitted for the four-cylinder King which had a grate area of 34·3 sq. ft, adhesion weight of 67½ tons and nominal tractive effort of 40,000 lbs. Was it practicable to match the King with a two-cylinder engine within the same space and limitations of weight?

A problem is to get something like the tractive effort of the King from two cylinders. Retaining the boiler pressure of 250 p.s.i. and the piston stroke of 28 in., the required cylinder diameter is $\sqrt{2}$ times that of the King, i.e. 23 in., which would be a shade too tight even in the Great Western loading gauge. A piston-stroke of 30 in. would bring this down only to 22·3 in. which, is not much better.

Brooding on this for a time we may remember that the King's nominal tractive effort of 40,000 lb. was just a publicity gesture. a politically necessary reply to the Southern *Lord Nelson*'s 33,500. For general purposes in British express-passenger-train service, a nominal tractive effort of about 1000 times the grate area is as high as is useful. The advantage of higher tractive effort is only that of raising the cylinder efficiency at speeds lower than the average.

So, aiming at tractive effort of about 35,000 lb. we find that cylinders 21 × 30 in. would suffice.

We have next to remember that the four-cylinder arrangement of the King enabled the reciprocating parts to be so well balanced that little hammer blow was added to the 68-ton adhesion weight. A two-cylinder engine is bound to be markedly different in generating considerable hammer blow. So somehow weight has got to be reduced.

The largest item in a steam locomotive is the boiler. The basic measure of its power is the grate area because that limits the combustion rate and there is a lower economic limit to the total heating surface through which the outgoing steam has received its heat. The only way of replacing the King boiler by a lighter one of the same power is to bring down the working pressure so that the thicknesses of plates, tube walls and firebox stays may be reduced. By redesigning the King boiler for 200 p.s.i. instead of 250, its weight of 25 tons might be reduced by about 3 tons, which is better than nothing. To obtain the nominal tractive effort of 35,000 lb. at

200 p.s.i. within a cylinder-diameter of 22 in., a piston-stroke of 33 in. is required. This is very shocking as even Churchward never went beyond 30 in., which was also shocking when he introduced it on the Great Western. But it was retained there, and in fifty years spread on to some 1400 locomotives.

The diameter of 22 in. for outside cylinders is unusual in British locomotives, but both the London & South Western and the London, Brighton & South Coast Railways used it and room could certainly be found for it in the slightly wider loading gauge of the Great Western Railway.

It may be remarked that the locomotives just mentioned were not distinguished flyers and the reason was that the valves were not big enough to feed the big cylinders with steam at an economical cut-off at high speed. To match the standard Saint in this respect, the 22 × 33 in. cylinders would need valves 12 in. in diameter with 2 in. lap.

To eliminate a bit of nonsense in the Kings, the Churchward standard wheel diameters of 3 ft 2 in. and 6 ft 8½ in. would be retained. This would give a nominal tractive effort of 33,600 lb. a sufficiently trifling advance on the Lord Nelson's 33,500 lb. to emphasize the absurdity of the tractive effort war in 1923–1927.

Hammer blow by the balance weights remains a problem. It can be reduced to any desired degree by reducing the rotating weights provided partially to balance the reciprocating members and this increases the fore-and-aft pounding at the driving axleboxes and therefore the pulsation of draw-bar pull on the tender and the train. The magnitude of these latter effects depends also on the elasticity of draw-bar springs. Fore-and-aft oscillation of the engine, and axlebox thump twice per revolution are fatiguing for the enginemen and this is something to be considered when examining the various possibilities at this stage in design.

Two cylinders (even 22 × 33) over the bogie are lighter than four spread about the engine in Great Western style and, moreover, the frame-and-cylinder construction can be much stiffer.

On p. 144 is shown such a King-size Saint as closely as possible in the Churchward style with Stephenson valve gear inside the frame. The combination of 22-in. cylinder and 12-in. valve requires the running board to be higher, in that vicinity, than that of the

King by an inch or two. The same circumstance arose in the Granges and Manors and was accommodated by a positive step in the running board. Advantage is taken of this precedent to get more station-platform clearance of the cylinder by raising its centre line above that of the driving axles and so justifying a worthwhile step in the running board.

The upper parts of the coupled wheels are hidden by a continuous splasher as applied to the King and Castle semi-streamlined in 1935 and to the Hawksworth 2/4-6-os ten years later. Such splashers are simpler to make, and by their long horizontal lines add to the appearance of the locomotive an impression of length and this is usually approved in anything to be associated with speed.

Would it be justifiable to retain inside valve gear merely because outside valve gear would conflict with Swindon tradition? The answer would have to be 'No!' if policy were sufficiently forward-looking to realize that locomotives were going to have to be more readily prepared for running than had been the case in the past. A locomotive that could be fully oiled without being run over a pit could on that account be more quickly got off the shed and on to the job than any that did require a pit. The former facility was therefore valuable and it meant that the engine should have no inside cylinder and no inside valve gear. So a really up-to-date super-Saint needed outside valve gear.

Use of Walschaerts valve gear requires the raised part of the running board to be extended and the result is shown on p. 144. The running board might of course have been extended at its highest level right back to the cab, but in the writer's view fully exposed wheels look crude and any near approach to that condition is nearly as bad.

The form of fire-grate used on Saints, Castles and Kings was not ideal because firemen found it useful to minimize entry of air to the firebox by running with a fire built high enough to block the lower half of the fire hole. This meant that the back part of the fire was so deep that the draught through it was weaker than it was in the front half of the box where most of the combustion therefore occurred. The remedy was to extend the slope of the grate right to the back so as to make it impossible to have the fire there more than about a foot deep. The record-breaking long fireboxes in France had this feature and they were commonly fired at high combustion rates.

Complaints in later years from enginemen about the fatiguing vibration on the footplates of out-of-condition two-cylinder engines at speed prompt one to wonder whether it might have been useful to mount the footplate on the tender, isolated from the worst vibration of the engine by a 'soft' spring in the connection between engine and tender. Consideration would have to be given to questions about clearance between footplate and cab sides on sharp curves and indeed one might wonder whether the cab itself could be mounted on the tender.

Reflection on the double handling of coal that was often regrettably necessary in Great Western tenders emphasizes the need in any rational design for accommodation of coal, right up to the limit of the loading gauge, right at the front of the tender. It must be presented to the fireman on the shovelling plate, seven feet above rail level, so that he does not have to lift it into the fire hole. What is the maximum weight of coal that can be self-trimming to a shovelling plate at that height? The answer is about 8 tons, provided that the most effective possible design is used. Care in loading the tender would have been required to achieve this maximum and even more care to ensure that the coal was entirely inside the loading gauge. In the rather carefree days after World War II, locomotive tenders on some British railways (not the Great Western) could often be seen piled with coal well above the nominal limit from overhead coaling plant which ought to have had substantial trimming plates to wipe off any excess as the locomotive moved away.

A high bunker immediately behind the cab prohibits use of the 12-ft long fire irons required to reach the front of a King-size grate unless special provision is made, in the form of a fire-iron container underneath the coal in the tender. When in this, the fire irons present their business ends to the fireman who can select the one he wants and can slide it out to enter the firehole directly without lifting or rotation. To get it back after use he needs tongs to handle the hot parts of it. In the ordinary way it was not necessary to use fire irons while the engine was in motion and this was fortunate as a

12-ft rod weighing half a hundredweight was awkward. Nevertheless rational design must facilitate this operation and under-coal parking (used on some European railways) of fire irons is advantageous.

The biggest disgrace in the operation of steam locomotives in Britain was the general absence of facilities for disposing of ash and smokebox char. The expense of ground equipment was the main obstacle; with that provided, each locomotive needed only a hopper-type ashpan and a char chute from the smokebox to make dumping of ash and char very quick and simple.

A general manager, having been told that a proposed King-size Saint would beat the Southern Lord Nelson by only a hundred pounds in nominal tractive effort, might be disposed to say that this was not good enough and that a bigger margin of superiority was required. What might the designer do to meet this demand?

The easiest thing was to say 'We can set the safety valves to blow off at 250 p.s.i. instead of 200, and the nominal tractive effort will then be about 43,000 lb. That should vanquish and discourage everybody. A new boiler and everything else would stand that pressure for a few weeks, and that would justify publicity about the 43,000 lb. Later on we can come down to the 200 p.s.i. that is all we need for the job.' With the reputation of the big Saint made in this way, later engines of the class could have been placed in service at 200 p.s.i. without any initial period at publicity level.

In examining the possible advantages of a King-size Saint over the actual King, one should remember that according to the very careful testing of No. 6001 in 1953, the internal resistance of the King was very much greater than one would have expected from corresponding information about comparable locomotives such as L M S Duchesses. It cannot be said that this circumstance was ever fully explained but it does tend to emphasize the fact that frictional losses in a four-cylinder engine are, in the nature of things, likely to be greater than those in a two-cylinder engine of the same power. So a few King-size Saints might well have been worth trying in comparison with Kings.

SUPER KING-SIZE SAINT

The British people have constantly been taunted about their excessive insularity and some enthusiastic students of British railway operation would admit, or even proclaim, that they had no interest in anything that happened on foreign railways. There was no reason why they *should* have any such interest if they didn't want to and indeed there was enough going on on British railways between World Wars I and II to keep enthusiasts on their toes. It was notable, therefore, that steam locomotive development in the early 1930s by André Chapelon on the Paris–Orleans Railway was so striking as to break down the insular reserve of many locomotive enthusiasts who had formerly confined themselves entirely to British steam.

Reactions were various to the performances of the Chapelon 4–8–0 rebuilds of Paris–Orleans Pacifics. Some disbelieved them. Some asked, 'Why can't we do the same in Britain?' Some said, 'We could do this if we wanted, but of course working as hard as that is bound to knock quick hell out of any engine!' Others, most impressed of all, travelled across to France to see, hear and feel for themselves. One enthusiast who rode for miles with his head out of the next coach to a hard-thrashed Chapelon 4–8–0, exerted every sense to get all he possibly could from this proximity. Some time after returning home he found his hair to be holding a lot of char from the chimney of the Chapelon Hercules. He proudly exhibited this unintentionally smuggled treasure to his friends with his personal guarantee that it had come through the tubes of No. 4711, adding (unnecessarily) that it had nothing to do with the widely advertised perfume of that designation.

It suffices here to say about Chapelon's work that it produced locomotives that could develop about 50 per cent more power than did British locomotives of comparable major dimensions. The 'fifty per cent rule' has been mentioned in connection with Brunel's broad gauge; a hundred years later its effect could be seen in messages from France.

Anyone who knew anything at all about locomotives was bound to be impressed on learning that a 100-ton locomotive with Chapelon modifications could produce 3000 draw-bar horsepower continuously whereas no British locomotive had been reliably tested at anything over 2000. How was it done? Why could not we do it here? Inevitably the fact that the French locomotives concerned had compound expansion, whereas the British had not, was assumed to be a big constituent of the miracle. In actual fact, the particular French locomotives were compounds simply because *most* big French locomotives were compounds anyway; it was, so to say, 'an old Spanish custom' to use compounds in France. Analysis of detailed figures showed that compounding could not have contributed much to the astounding performances of the Chapelon locomotives as they were produced at low expansion ratios well within the economical range of single expansion.

The essence of the Chapelon method was simply to urge the fire very much harder than was deemed reasonable in Britain and to make the cylinders big enough to use the big steam flow economically at the ordinary running speed. The nub of the Chapelon method was to design the boiler so that it could work at very high combustion rates without letting any exceptionally high fraction of the fire's heat get away into the smokebox. The drill was to fit the firebox with a thermic syphon to catch more of the heat there by radiation (which involves no friction of gas on metal) and to get more heating surface per unit length of fire tube by providing it with internal longitudinal ribs on the Serve principle. There is a weight penalty for this (you never get anything for nothing) but nevertheless the power-weight ratio is increased and Chapelon locomotives were world-beaters in this respect.

To produce the necessary strong draught on the fire without undue back pressure on the pistons Chapelon used a double chimney, with each of the two blast nozzles subdivided into quarters.

To use the expected extra 50 per cent of steam economically an extra 50 per cent of cylinder volume was required. This may be expressed in another way by saying that the nominal tractive effort needed to be about 50 per cent higher than usual in relation to the grate area. So the basic essentials in attempting to emulate Chapelon were clear.

If the General Manager had been impressed by reports of the

amazing powers developed by Chapelon-style locomotives in France he might well ask the Chief Mechanical Engineer whether he could 'do a Chapelon' with one of the King-size Saints. What modifications might be necessary for this?

Firstly a thermic syphon in the firebox and an increase in tube-heating surface by using more tubes of smaller diameter.

Secondly a double blast pipe to get stronger draught with not much increase in back-pressure.

Thirdly a 50-per-cent increase in nominal tractive effort.

The first change means a heavier boiler. The second change also means a small increase in weight but there is no other serious difficulty.

The third change could be achieved simply by raising the working pressure from 200 to 300 p.s.i. but everything would need to be strengthened and so the boiler in particular would have to be much heavier on top of the weight increase demanded by the first change.

Alternatively the third change might be achieved by adding a third cylinder without increase in boiler pressure.

It is to be considered whether by setting back the leading coupled axle, and by using a short connecting rod for the inside cylinder, the latter can be located where its piston-rod gland can be reached by a man standing on the track inside the frame and reaching over the trailing bogie axle.

This could in fact be done by moving the leading coupled axle by 1 ft, making its distance from the main driving axle 7 ft, and so the standard 7-ft coupling rods could be used.

The inside connecting rod would be 6 ft long and this is not too short to go with 26 in. stroke. To make the swept volume of the inside cylinder equal to that of the outside ones, so that all three torque impulses are equal, the diameter of the inside cylinder would be

$$22\sqrt{(33/26)} = 24\cdot8$$

As the cylinder volumes are equal, the same 12 $\times$ 2 in piston-valve size is right for all three.

By far the most convenient way of working the inside valve is from the outside valves by a Holcroft conjugating mechanism (see p. 101) ahead of the cylinders. The way to avoid trouble from conjugating mechanism B is to make it stiff for its weight and to keep its bearings regularly grease-gunned.

The numerous pins in the conjugating mechanism ahead of the cylinders would each have a 'rolling bearing' which means that the load itself would be taken through rollers, balls or needles. For these, grease-gun lubrication is ideal in that it keeps dirt out and in that daily attention is an unskilled operation.

A hole in each frame plate ahead of the cylinders gives ample access for grease-gunning the pins in the conjugating mechanism. Periodic examination of the inside valve could be made after extracting it from the rear of the steam chest.

This engine has mechanism inside the frame but it can be reached without using a pit and there is so little of it that once he has ducked under the frame plate behind a rear bogie wheel a man can stand upright and work on the mechanism as easily as if it were outside the frame.

An alternative would be to fit two $15\frac{1}{2}$ in. inside cylinders and this would have slight advantages over the three-cylinder scheme. On the other hand, it would restrict both the width of the axle-boxes on the crank axle and the space available for a man to work between the frame plates.

Item c on p. 144 shows how such a three-cylinder locomotive might look. On occasions when the combination of load and schedule demanded power appreciably beyond the ordinary maximum expected of a standard King, a second fireman could help in bringing out the extra 50 per cent in power and at the same time so lighten the work of the regular fireman that he might welcome the overload thus divided between two men.

The double chimney shown on p. 144 is not so tall as it might have been but even the small extension of $2\frac{1}{2}$ in. to the overall height of 13 ft has an extraordinary effect in making the locomotive itself look less imposing.

No British railway ever did produce a locomotive specifically intended to work at Chapelon intensity as no normal duty required such effort from the class of locomotive ordinarily used for it. Some Chapelon-style locomotives might, however, have been used for the hardest jobs so that a reserve of load capacity was available for emergencies. The four Gresley Pacifics that had double chimneys before 1939 might be regarded as being examples of high-power reserves, but their allocation in service did not suggest any background plan of this kind.

Double chimneys were not applied to Great Western locomotives until after World War II and their effect was discernible in the attainment of higher top speeds in easy running conditions rather than in higher power when pulling hard.

Note: To provide inscriptions for the name plates of the speculative King-size Saints shown on p. 144 it seemed reasonable to seek saints who were also kings. These are not numerous, but three were discovered and this sufficed for the purpose.

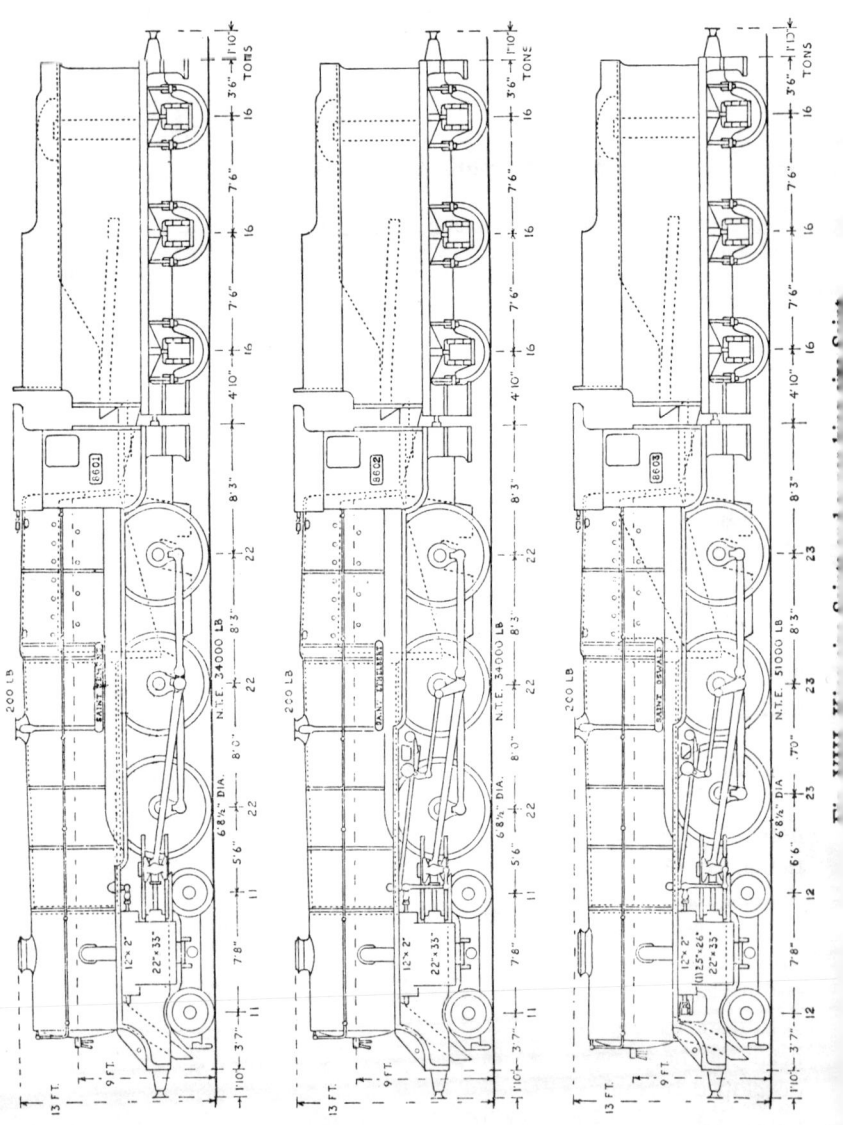

CHAPTER 10

On the Road

TORTURED SAINT

It is my good fortune in writing this book that I have been able to draw on the notebooks of two old friends, the late Mr G. H. W. Clifford and the late Mr E. K. Harrison. As different as can be imagined in all other respects, these enthusiasts were as one in the intensity of devotion to the steam locomotive and all that went with her. The former, modest and retiring to a degree, was a penetrating observer and a shrewd judge of the quality of what was done in the design, building, operation and maintenance of steam locomotives.

Mr E. K. Harrison excelled in beguiling enginemen to permit him to make unofficial journeys on locomotives. Beginning at the age of six in the West Country and ending at the age of eighty-three on the electrified line between Sheffield and Manchester, his 'black-market' footplate riding extended to some 70,000 miles over most of Great Britain. At one time or another he drove and fired locomotives of at least two classes on every British railway. His notes on his railway experiences were extensive and unconventional. At various times he submitted articles for publication but editors were not appreciative, just horrified. Harrison's articles were simply live narratives, different from the stodgy suet of Edwardian journalism and entirely lacking in smarm. Edwardian enthusiasts would have wondered what had hit them.

Editors were probably right in refusing to put ideas into the heads of their readers. A harmless style of journalism had been developed by cutting down to size those who would have maintained Victorian exuberance, and there was no point in disturbing readers' equanimity by hinting that thrills on British railways had not ended with the 1895 Race to the North. Convinced that it was just waste of effort to repeat anything more remarkable than the previous best, Harrison limited his appreciation of notable happenings to heavy marks in his notebooks. These in conjunction with the memories of verbatim accounts by Harrison of his experiences enable one to get some quite vivid impressions of what locomotives could do when really put to it. Although a great deal has been published over the years about hard running in ordinary service it is more than probable that many of the highest spots were missed.

Harrison was one of the very few footplate observers who ever thought of making any numerical estimate of the fireman's work. This was probably because he had done a lot of it himself, and this was because he was really interested in what kept engines going. Not for him the leisurely role of a non-productive note-taker on the footplate; he liked to be doing a bit to recompense the men for their kindness in having him or to reconcile whichever of them would have preferred not to have had him. But where he was unable to help with the physical work he did at least make a note of how much of it was done. He felt that he ought at least to take that much trouble.

Harrison was sure that many of the best engine performances were never recorded and it was his policy to be prepared at all times to take a train that seemed likely to make a harder run than usual. He was, however, always prepared to be disappointed; the actual outcome of an emergency might easily turn out to be opposite to what one hoped. A main-line engine failed and had to be replaced hurriedly at an intermediate station. What would the enginemen do on the remainder of the journey? Set out to regain the lost time? Or just say, 'We're late now and nobody will expect us to pick up any time with a crock like this, so let's take it easy.'

But Harrison was once lucky enough to drop on a strange emergency at Paddington. He never found out what the real origin of it was, and perhaps it doesn't matter. The outcome was remarkable enough and it was sheer good luck that Harrison happened to be on the spot and was able, by dint of enterprise and hardihood, to make the most of the situation.

Being in the neighbourhood with some time to spare, he had

gone into Paddington Station to see the down Limited go out at 10.30 a.m. and perhaps also the departure of the 10.45. Many people have done this kind of thing at various times and have found themselves watching the 3.30 p.m. go before being forced to the conclusion that it really was time they went themselves. The first remarkable thing about the occasion of this particular visit of Harrison to the main departure platform was that at 10.30 a.m. the Limited was all packed up and ready to go except that there was no engine at the front end of it. Alongside where the engine should should have been was a knot of officials looking impatient, frustrated and important. Obviously the engine was to be expected at any minute and the easiest thing was to wait for it. A common artifice in cases of this sort was to do a quick shuffle and use for the vacant job an engine scheduled for a later train. But there was always a lot of fuss about anything of that sort. If the substitute engine turned out to be a poor one the engine driver would make a caustic report about it. If it turned out to be a good one, the people who should have had it complained about having it taken from them and wondered when, if ever, they would get it back on its proper 'turns'. And on this day, likely as not, there would be no enginemen at Paddington or near it who knew the road to Plymouth or would feel confident about running the Limited with a substitute engine. Anyway they did wait, getting more exasperated every minute – and no wonder. For the Limited to be 'late away' was almost unknown. For there to be no engine for it five, six, seven, eight . . . ten minutes after 10.30 was incredible. The departure side of the station seemed to stiffen into shocked rigidity (so Harrison told me) and there was a deathly hush in the place. If the Great Western had used pop safety valves there wouldn't have been a hush; you would have been able to hear the noise down on the Metropolitan line.

When they had started to fix it for the 10.45 to go, the engine for the Limited came rather hurriedly into sight. The very first thing that Harrison noticed was that it was not a Castle – he could tell that from the shape of the cab roof. When it got closer still, he could see that it wasn't even a Star, but a Saint. From that instant his senses quickened. A Saint for the Limited with fourteen on and going to be a quarter of an hour late away!

Harrison was quick, imaginative and resourceful, and while the reception committee gathered round the footplate and the driver backed the Saint up to the train, he looked up and down the platform and by the grace of God, no less, he saw just what he wanted close at hand – one of those old hefty wooden boxes with internal compartments to accommodate ginger-beer bottles. With one unhesitating movement Harrison picked it up and shoved it into the front van.

Then he went and joined the throng to hear some of the row that was going on. A couple of men, besides the crew, had come from Old Oak on the engine and they joined the platform staff in a kind of profane exhortation to the driver to do something he was stoutly disinclined to do. His soft West-country burr was in marked contrast to the strident whines of the Cockneys and even his swear-words didn't sound bad.

Vituperation and the like continued as the ejector built up the vacuum and, as the blower was on quite briskly and the safety valves blowing off, it was rather a mob scene for Paddington. It was more like Euston with a George all set to blast up to Camden and not a bit like Victoria with a Stroudley Gladstone about to totter out with four coaches, first stop East Croydon.

They got the 'right away', the driver made an ill-tempered 'pop' from the whistle and opened the regulator. Harrison started his split-second chronograph ('stop-watch' he used to call it) and, behind the rest of the crowd on the platform, got into the front van and shut the door before anyone else had realized what had happened. He did not record any details about the first coach, but he had worked out, from the moment his interest had been awakened, that he should station himself on the right-hand side so that he might see as much as possible of the interior of the engine cab.

You couldn't see very much behind a tender well loaded with coal, but what you could see was the reversing handle and Harrison wanted to see that, right from the word 'go' to whatever word was used at Plymouth North Road. He knew that the driver would be sure to start from rest in full gear and he figured that if he never took his eye off the double handle all the way to Plymouth and counted the turns and fractions of turns, plus or minus, made by the driver he could deduce the reading of the cut-off indicator at every point of the journey.

The position of the mounting of the reversing screw on the Saints has been criticized on various grounds, but one thing could be said for it. A really determined passenger in the front coach could keep track of the cut-off setting if he didn't mind leaning well out of the right-hand side of the vehicle and if he was willing and able to keep his mind and his eye on the job absolutely all the time.

I suppose a good many young students of the steam locomotive have made observations on regulator opening and reversing-gear setting on all sorts of locomotives with low tenders from vantage points on leading coaches. (The Lancashire & Yorkshire o–6–os with highly-pitched boilers were marvellous for this and of course especially when they hadn't much coal on the tender. By leaning out of the top half of an end door of a coach immediately behind the tender you could see everything the men did. I never heard whether *they* liked this facility for passengers.) But it is one thing to study the adjustments of throttle and cut-off in the acceleration from rest to normal running speed, and it is quite another matter to continue to do so for about four hours on end. But there it was. Old Harrison was a toughish bird, he always had goggles with him – as he used to say, 'You never know' – it was not a cold day and an epic was quite on the cards. Things like lunch and his appointments for the afternoon would have to wait. You really did commit yourself when you got on to the Limited. It was no use changing your mind after half an hour and wishing you hadn't come. If you were in the main part of the train, you were stuck there till nearly twenty to three.

This didn't bother Harrison. He leaned out on the right and listened to the old Saint blast her way out of Paddington and down the hill to Royal Oak. The train was so long that the engine was round most of the bend in Platform 1 before she started and she had got into the straight before the driver notched her up and Harrison saw what he did without any trouble. When the reversing handle was horizontal the outer end of it was just about flush with the cab side and a passenger could see it without leaning out very much. Provided you didn't lose count you could always know what the setting was to half a turn; if you really did lean out you could tell to a quarter of a turn.

Harrison couldn't expect to see the setting of the regulator handle – at least until a lot of the coal had gone – but on this trip he soon gained the impression that this would not matter at all. It seemed that in the first furlong the driver lifted the regulator handle right up so that the upper quadrant arm banged on the open stop and then, because it wouldn't go any further, he fastened it up with a loop of string. (This was before they put balance weights on the handles.)

The driver was in no hurry to notch up and the engine blasted out to Old Oak in a way that surprised even Harrison who was used to rough work. This was most unusual and the old story was that anything of this kind was just idiotic because it would tear great holes in a carefully prepared fire. With my tongue in my cheek I mentioned this to Harrison in discussing this trip with him, and all he could say was that if any holes were torn in the fire, the fireman must have bunged them up pretty quick with good solid lumps of coal.

They didn't work by any book on this trip. There had evidently been a pretty tense situation at the shed and at Paddington and on the engine on the way. The Saint was not the originally intended engine for the job and the driver was furious about something. The way in which he drove out of Paddington was that of a man working a bit of mad off. This was all very human and understandable but the marvellous thing about this man was that he still seemed to have some mad to work off on Dainton bank down in Devon, over three hours later. What a man! And what a fireman! And what a dear, bashable, uncomplaining Saint! You could tell she had taken a bashing. The back of the copper rim of her chimney was black and blue with heat long before she got to Plymouth.

By the time they had got through Southall in less than twelve minutes with fifteen on, Harrison could sense an epic coming. He had quickly fixed himself up to take a full record and he was glad he had. He used to clip to his left arm a board that carried notebook and watch so that he could note times and other things while holding on with his left hand. He did not prepare beforehand any list of timing points, but simply noted the times of happenings as they happened. He left till afterwards the sorting out of information for different purposes. On the run he noted everything that might be useful but made no attempt to deduce anything from it as that could be done later. On the run he did nothing that could be done later as that might have caused him to miss opportunities that would not return.

Anyone who has ever ridden on a locomotive making anything like a hard run knows that the firing is the measure of the job. Any worthwhile record must include some indication of what the fireman did and the obviously easy way of doing this was to note the shovelfuls of coal and the times when they were fed into the firebox. There was no point in recording the times in split seconds or in imagining that coal consumption could be deduced with any precision (a shovelful on Dainton bank at ten to two in the afternoon tended to be smaller than a shovelful at Hanwell at twenty to eleven in the morning, but it felt heavier) but the figures did give some idea of how hard the fireman worked and how he had to respond to the running of the engine. A footplate-riding observer who really wanted to make the most of his opportunities would clearly concentrate on significant occurrences that could not readily be observed from the train.

To Harrison, who knew his stuff, it was obvious that this epic – if that was what it was really going to be – would depend entirely on the fireman and that some record of his work was very highly desirable. He had, of course, thought about this many years before and had proved to his own satisfaction that he could count the shovelfuls by observing the steam-cloud by day and the glow of the fire by night. (Every time a shovelful of coal was added to the fire, the light on the steam-cloud was cut down drastically and the efflux from the chimney went dark for a moment.) So you didn't *have* to be on the footplate to count the shovel strokes. If you didn't mind having your head out of the window and you were really interested in the working of the locomotive you could learn something.

Old Harrison was well up on all this and set out to write down all he could possibly observe on this trip or at least as far as he could last out. Fortunately it was a warmish day. This made the steam cloud less intense so that the smoke showed up better than usual although you still had to see what was happening at the chimney-top or just above it. And of course you didn't have to wrap your face up so tightly for a long run in warm weather as you did when it was really cold.

Obviously Harrison would note times at stations and at junction signal-boxes but what about local maximum and minimum speeds? For these he used rail-point timing at particular places and might have had to let the shovelful record slip in such vicinities. So he set himself for four hours of concentration on a strict routine. When the coal heap had gone down a bit he might have found it useful to stand on the ginger-beer-bottle box to see a bit more of what was going on on the footplate, but in the early stages he might just as well have stood on the floor with his head out in what the early aviators might have called the 'slip stream' but which could be more accurately termed the 'grit stream'.

I don't suppose Harrison would have pursued his plan for very long if he had not had goggles because he would have been blind for half the time, but as it was he had almost a good word to say for the grit. He could very nearly count the shovelfuls by the variations in grit flow. Every time a loaded shovel entered the fire hole of a working locomotive all the dust and fine grit was swept up by the draught and shot out of the chimney. So a sensitive skin could count the shovelfuls even if the eyes had been put out of action by grit.

Old Harrison noted this with sardonic satisfaction and the pages of his notebook were grubby enough to confirm all his petulant comments on this part of his self-imposed task. Students of the steam locomotive in action may well feel grateful to Harrison for his enterprise and fortitude in recording so much of what was done by No. 2922 on this occasion.

With his head out of the window Harrison had the full benefit of noise from the exhaust. Out to Southall, where they were really going, the chatter from the chimney was devilish, but Harrison was coming to realize that it was going to keep on like that all the way to Sonning anyhow. It was a notably even beat, like that made by a boy pressing a stick on closely spaced iron railings as he runs past them. It might have been called a pretty beat in recognition of its evenness but the adjective was quite wrong for anything of such harsh ferocity. Harrison was delighted but he wondered how long it could go on because of course it took a lot of coal to keep it up.

In the ordinary way one would have said that a Saint would have a hard job to keep Limited time with fourteen on and one could hardly expect a driver to try to do more than that. The circumstances were, however, obviously quite special and getting through Southall inside twelve minutes proved that the driver had something special in mind. So Harrison resolved that he would get everything he could down on paper. What was happening might turn out to be only a flash in the first pan but never mind, if he kept on recording times and shovelfuls there would be no regret afterwards.

He could see that the old Saint was a bit lively in her movements and that the driver was getting his share of the '29 bend' as her back end swayed and he could see that the fireman was hard at it. It took Harrison all his time to record the shovel strokes let alone make them.

The driver had left the reversing handle horizontal so that Harrison could see it without too much trouble and it looked as if he was not going to move it, at least till he got past Reading. Harrison thought that the cut-off was about 35 per cent (he did not make much effort to estimate it closely at that stage) and the engine was really being thrashed at that when doing 70 or so. Could she keep it up?

While Harrison was asking himself this question she started to blow off! So the question really was, for how far could the fireman keep it up? If they had been going to Bristol it would be all right if he kept it up for 80 miles or so to Wootton Bassett, but on the way to Plymouth you had to get to Whiteball – 150 miles – before you could really let up. Harrison formed the opinion that the driver would either have to ease up to give the fireman some relief or, of course, do some of the firing himself. Harrison hoped he would, because it looked as if the engine could take the thrashing and so if the men would keep her hard at it there was a good chance of doing an epic.

So they roared along the old main line, Harrison rather glad that

Brunel's broad gauge had left plenty of room between the up and down main lines of standard gauge because that made it less dangerous to keep his head out when they met up trains. I don't think I would have risked it myself as it only takes 5 seconds to pass a 15-coach train when both you and it are doing seventy, but as Harrison said, the driver might decide to give his reversing screw an odd turn during that 5 seconds and if you miss it you've lost your reference position and your cut-off record will then be more difficult to draw up.

The driver kept her going all the way to Reading gasworks before cutting her down to drifting steam. He did not move the reversing handle. If the cut-off was indeed at about 35 per cent as Harrison estimated, it was about right for drifting, and drift she did. She was running so fast as she came to Reading Station that Harrison hoped that the driver had remembered which way they were going. He had, in fact, remembered and he put the brakes on hard enough for the train to pull back on the engine but not hard enough to make a lot of difference to the speed. Harrison was not very happy about it but they got round the west curve all right and the driver let drifting steam run the train on to Southcote Junction. They went through it 'running well', as the saying is.

I asked Harrison afterwards whether it would be right to say, in any account of this run, that it was characterized by scrupulous observance of speed restrictions. He replied that you could say it if you liked but that as a matter of fact the driver just let the bagger go.

After Southcote the driver opened her up again – to full regulator, Harrison was sure it must have been – and then the fireman took his place against the reversing gear. Harrison was relieved and delighted at this. The driver had taken over the firing which went on just as fast as before and for him to have done so at this early stage in the journey suggested that he was aiming to keep on bashing for some time yet.

The fireman disappeared as they came to Aldermaston troughs and Harrison pulled his window up just in case there should be a bad overfill. But all went well and Harrison was soon out again counting dark spurts from the chimney.

Then for repeated short periods there was no one looking ahead on the right-hand side of the engine. Harrison thought that the fireman was breaking coal while his mate kept on shovelling. As they came to Newbury the driver reappeared on the right-hand side and gave the reversing screw about half a turn. On the steepening gradients up to Savernake Harrison had to expect some readjustments of cut-off and so he watched specially carefully on this stretch.

They were doing over a mile a minute from Newbury, but speed was dropping and by Kintbury the driver was beginning to move the reversing screw, a few notches at a time, and although the Saint pulled harder and the blast came stronger, the gradient took its toll and the fireman sweated on with – one may be sure – no time for even a glance at the serene countryside that they were spraying with grit. It was a spectacle of steam and speed such as Turner had no chance of seeing; had he done so he might also have noticed the smoke. Harrison certainly continued to do so and to think of the fireman, without dropping his glance from the reversing handle.

The last three furlongs to Savernake Summit are at 1 in 106, which is a bit unfair, and the Saint was barking bad-temperedly as the driver shoved her into 50 per cent for that last bit. He held it at that for another mile while speed built up and then put it at about 35 per cent for the next 25 miles down to Westbury.

In the meantime the fireman had used the short period of low speed near the summit to climb up on to the heap of coal and to shove some of it down to the front. Those low Great Western tenders were all right behind Dean singles burning about 25 lb. a mile but when you were going all the way to Plymouth and thrashing a Saint they were not good enough. Nearly half the coal had to be handled twice and the job of fetching it from the back of the tender while the train was running was awkward, hard and risky. Of course, firemen could get used to it and could do it so nonchalantly that non-professional footplate reporters never even noticed it.

But Harrison had realized that if they kept on punching the engine the way they'd done it out to Savernake, a lot of fetching would have to be done before they got to Brent. He began to wonder whether this might set a limit to what could be achieved. Indeed it would have done so, except for the fact that the driver worked as hard on the firing as the fireman did. Fired (as it were) by resentment about something that had happened at Old Oak, they toiled like demons on this trip and the poor old Saint had to take it.

Harrison had time to notice that they had picked up a minute on the booked time of $69\frac{1}{2}$ minutes from Paddington to Bedwyn and this was hard running for a Saint. It showed that the enginemen were really trying and suggested that they were not likely to waste any time on the next stretch; nor did they.

Over the 10 miles to Patney, generally downhill but with some adverse bits, they averaged 70 or so, and then kept tearing away on the 6 miles of sharper downhill to Lavington. Harrison got a bit scared over this. The line is not exactly straight and it was the practice to give engines not much more than drifting steam down there, but this driver kept the Saint pulling hard down the hill and so the speed went up and up with the engine rasping, rolling and swaying in quite alarming fashion. Harrison didn't like it at all, but continued to do his stuff and was not surprised to find on examining his figures afterwards that they touched 90 in the mile below Lavington Station. At Edington they were down to 70 and were doing 74 when the driver shut off and jammed the brakes on pretty hard for the slow running through Westbury, where the fireman did a quick bit of coal-trimming on the tender.

There they had picked up $3\frac{1}{2}$ minutes on the hardest part of the Limited schedule. A hope arose in Harrison's mind. Was the driver going to try to pick up 15 minutes? Was there a bet on, or something? Had somebody told him that he couldn't time the Limited with a Saint? Was he out to show them a thing or two? He'd certainly shown them something already and as anybody could pick up a minute or two from Castle Cary to Taunton, there was no knowing what might be done by this man. Harrison was already glad he'd come on this train. He was by now standing by to be delighted.

Harrison was not prepared to swear that they came down to 30 m.p.h. in passing through Westbury, but the Weymouth part was slipped there and the driver then opened out as if he were in a great hurry to get to Taunton where they were due to drop two more coaches.

Harrison got ready to draw back from the window as they picked up water from the Westbury trough; he had been splashed once or twice by the fireman's spray pipe and he didn't want to get any wetter. For his purpose it was vital that he should see exactly what the driver did with the reversing handle on the next 13 miles to the summit at Mile Post 122¾.

From the approach to Westbury through Frome, over Brewham (M.P. 122¾) and down to Castle Cary where there is another speed restriction, was a messy bit of line. In 1933, when the Westbury cut-off and the Frome cut-off were opened, this length was transformed but before then it was a pest, and the time made over it depended, as much as anything, on the way the driver ran through the stations at Westbury and Frome. They were both nominally restricted to 30 m.p.h. and some trains undoubtedly came down to that speed, but others certainly did not. Harrison thought that the Saint didn't, but he took no specific observation on the point. He was more interested in the movements of the reversing handle and in the smoke puffs. The engine was pushed hard to cover the 7·2 miles from Frome to the M.P. 122¾ top in 10 minutes and the fireman trimmed the coal so that none showed above the coping plate on the top of the tender. By standing on his box and craning out, Harrison could from there see everything in the cab more than 4 ft above the footplate.

It was quite a relief to Harrison to find that he could now count shovelfuls by the movements of the head of whoever was firing at the time. Such movements were much more clearly defined than smoke puffs, but on the other hand, standing on the box was less restful than standing on the floor. It was an embarrassing choice for Harrison, not eased by the fact that he would much rather have sat on the box and taken it easy. But he realized that he was on what looked like being the hottest Saint effort of the century and that it was up to him to get all the details he could. Keeping a constant watch on the reversing handle was quite wearing; there was absolutely no possibility of sitting down. The real miracle was that no ticket inspector or guard came along to bother him. He could have coped very ably (and even persuaded the intruder to bring him a cup of tea!) but while he was doing so, sure as fate, the driver would alter the cut-off.

From 30 m.p.h. at M.P. 122¾ to a 50 m.p.h. slack at Castle Cary in 6 minutes for 6·8 miles meant some pretty lively running and braking, with a quarter mile at 84. Old Harrison, toughish bird though he was, was a bit uneasy about this, and was surprised by what followed.

For after getting through Castle Cary the driver, who had evidently been chafing against all these speed restrictions in 20 miles, decided it was time they got going again. He set the cut-off at something like 40 per cent and set the fireman to watch the road while he himself did the firing on to Cogload Junction.

The poor old Saint had stood plenty of thrashing already, but now she got thrashed at speed. The road has plenty of curves and is a stretch where drivers usually run pretty quietly, but not on this trip! Harrison was thrilled by the way the exhaust crackled from the chimney at over 80, but he thought it was really wicked to treat any engine like that, and indeed perhaps a bit daft with over 100 miles to run.

The driver was not sparing himself either as the shovelfuls were going in at over five a minute, which was faster than it was over any other 27 miles of the journey.

I asked Harrison whether there was a ruddy glow from the cab as they went through Somerton tunnel and he said, 'No! There was no ruddy glow; it was ruddy well white, and so were the ruddy sparks, especially the ones that bounced off my forehead. Man, it was just God-awful. Talk about driving flat out! I hoped the driver knew what he was doing. I couldn't think how the engine could stand it for more than a minute or two.'

But everything held together and no bearings got over-hot in 27 miles of what was probably the hardest driving and the hottest firing that any Saint ever took.

Harrison was getting his share of the punishment also, as hot stuff of all sizes was coming out of the chimney and he thought his face was stopping rather too much of it. But even amongst all this, his mind did wander on to other things. He told me that he never passed Athelney without thinking of King Alfred and the cakes, and someone's idea of the headlines that the incident would have made in an American newspaper:

ALF GETS HIS

King cops a rough-house for letting cookies burn

Saint Gabriel was catching a rough-house all right, but as they ran on to the old main line at Cogload Junction the driver took his proper place on the footplate and notched her up from 40 to about 33 per cent, presumably to have a bit of an 'easy' before tackling Wellington bank. Harrison wondered whether the driver had intended to notch up a mile or two after Castle Cary but forgot to do it in his concentration on firing, and so gave himself a rougher spell than he intended.

Harrison remarked that 'all the way from Castle Cary, old *Gabriel* had been trumpeting like one o'clock' and oddly enough it must have been just about 1 p.m. when the driver eased up near Cogload.

They overdid things in picking up water at Creech and Harrison would have been unlucky if he had not been ready to whip his window up at the first hint of an overflow.

They must have been glad to drop two more coaches at Taunton, but they still had over 380 tons to pull up to Whiteball.

After passing Norton Fitzwarren, Harrison glanced back at the passing time at Taunton and with a bit of subtraction found that this incredible crew and this seemingly unbreakable engine had gained nearly 9 minutes on schedule. It struck him as they passed Victory Siding that victory might well be coming into sight. There was actually a chance that they would make Plymouth on time!

A mile or two farther on and Harrison started to doubt this as the driver seemed to be relaxing a bit. Speed was naturally dropping on the steepening grades, but the cut-off was not advanced beyond 40 per cent till after Wellington, where the 1 in 90 starts. After that it was moved to a maximum of about 50 per cent and speed gradually came down to 30 m.p.h. maintained on the last half mile up to the entrance to Whiteball tunnel. They had actually taken it fairly easily up the bank, as $13\frac{1}{2}$ minutes from Taunton to Whiteball is not fast, although the load was a heavy one for the steep pitch above Wellington.

Over the last stretch the fireman concentrated on getting coal forward from the back of the tender, leaving the fire to burn down as no great depth would be required over the 40 easy miles from Whiteball to Newton.

Once well out of the tunnel at Whiteball it was 'highball for Exeter'. The driver notched up to about 25 per cent and let her go as fast as she liked down to Cowley Bridge. She touched 80-odd here and there, rolling a bit, and the fireman had an easy time handling only three or four shovelfuls a minute. This was his rest period.

After slacking through Exeter and dropping two coaches the driver gave her a burst at about 35 per cent to pick up speed again, but then went back to 25 per cent for the winding level stretch on to Newton. They still had 310 tons, which was more than a Saint was supposed to take from Newton, and Harrison just had to hope that no busybody would take it into his silly head to stop them at Newton for a pilot. He guessed the enginemen would not ask for one.

He glanced at some of his figures and found that they had been inside even time all the way from Somerton and looked like keeping inside till after Newton. From Starcross to Dawlish the fireman was in the tender, but then he started piling plenty on the fire because the blast was going to pull hard on it when they got on to Dainton bank.

They did not slow down any more than was absolutely necessary at Newton Abbott and then the old girl was really hammered out to Aller, over the points round the first bend and up the winding grades to Stoneycombe, with the driver dropping the cut-off a few notches at a time till she was nearly in full gear for the last half mile. What solid, clean-clipped beats from the chimney! What a succession of hard, dry square blocks from the blast pipe! What a dynamic din in Dainton Tunnel as *Saint Gabriel* dragged her load up to it at nearly 30! Harrison was glad he'd come, if only to see and hear a Saint defy her tormentors and come up smiling after 200 miles of remorseless thrashing.

Newton to Dainton in 6 minutes meant very hard going for a Saint with 310 tons and they were now outside even time and were

a. No. 1016 (W91) *County of Hants*, Hawksworth County.

. No. 4388 (W96) in early days with copper-capped chimney.

. No. 4283 (W101). Note large balance weights.

. No. 7206 (W103) converted from (W101). Longest and heaviest class of Great Western locomotive.

not to get back inside it as curves alone prohibit fast running anywhere west of Newton.

They had gained $11\frac{1}{2}$ minutes on schedule at Dainton and $12\frac{1}{2}$ at Totnes less than 5 miles farther on, and so the driver must have let her run quite gaily in between. They came through Totnes at quite a bit over 60 and although the engine took yet another beating up to Brent, and blasted her protests to high heaven, they dropped half a minute on the scheduled time of $9\frac{1}{2}$ minutes for this 7 miles of gruelling grades. Another $2\frac{1}{2}$ miles of pounding up to Wrangaton and then everyone could relax. Drifting steam, with touches of the brakes here and there, was all that was required to keep the job going to Hemerdon and then after a wild plunge down the bank some very strong braking was required to come down from 75 m.p.h. to something more reasonable for the curving final stretch.

Old Harrison told me that he didn't know about anybody else, but he was glad to catch sight of the Cattewater and the pull up to Mutley tunnel. He'd stuck at that window for four hours and was ready to call it a day, but he still had two vital things to do. He had to note the stopping time and to count the turns of the reversing handle as the driver set her back to ease up for uncoupling and he was quite likely to do this immediately after stopping. So Harrison ended his vigil by getting off the train before it actually stopped and was abreast of the footplate when it did.

He watched the driver put her into back gear and was delighted to notice that he banged the nut right up to the stop because that gave Harrison (knowing how many turns there were in the full range) a good check on his natural assumption that she had started out of Paddington in full forward gear.

An obvious railway official of some kind came up to the engine and, all ears, so did Harrison.

'By God, Bill!' this man said. 'You've been tearin' a bit, haven't you?'

'No,' said the driver. 'We've come in very easy from Wrangaton.'

'Oh ay, but what about getting to Wrangaton?'

'Well, we pushed her a bit on the banks back along.'

'I'll bet you did. I expect you've knocked hell out of her. She'll want new brasses everywhere, I suppose.'

'Oh no, she's all right! I'll take her back to London tomorrow if you like.'

By this time she was uncoupled, the fireman had put a lamp on the back of the tender and the board was off. As *Saint Gabriel* went ahead to clear the way for the Penzance engine, the driver called to the inspector,

'Don't forget to wire Old Oak, "DOWN LIMITED RIGHT TIME NORTH ROAD".'

Looking at his watch now for the normal purpose of finding what time it was, Harrison observed that it was 2.37 p.m., exactly the time the Limited was due to arrive. Very satisfactory! And then he remembered that it had started 15 minutes late! Just try to think of picking up 15 minutes with 14 on out of Paddington. It was more than an epic. It was a miracle, or as that dreadful man Churchward might have said, a bloody miracle.

SEVERN TUNNEL SEE-SAW

The Severn Tunnel is said to be the longest underwater railway tunnel in the world but that circumstance did nothing to endear it to the staff responsible for running steam-hauled goods trains through it. It is a V-shaped depression and as that type of profile presented special difficulties to the crews of loose-coupled goods trains, it is a miracle that no serious accident has happened in it.

After such a train had been cautiously let down to the bottom under the restraint of brakes on the engine(s) and tender(s) and perhaps also on the guard's van, the slack had to be taken gently out of the wagon couplings as the engine began to climb the up-grade. This had to be done very carefully as there was otherwise a risk of breaking a coupling and in unlucky circumstances this may occur in a way that can derail a wagon and perhaps most of the train so that the adjacent line is also blocked. If a train were to come along that line at speed the consequences could be frightful. Collisions are bad enough anywhere but confinement to a tunnel could make matters much worse. Happily there has been no serious accident of this kind in the Severn Tunnel and this is a tribute to unremitting care in the handling of the thousands of loose-coupled goods trains that have been taken through. Because the speed of such trains was strictly limited in the interest of safety, they could not 'take a run' at the climb out of the tunnel. The locomotives had therefore to work very hard at low speed and, despite the forced ventilation system, visibility in their wake might be cut down by smoke to a few yards.

In the early days the whole length of the tunnel formed a single block section some 4½ miles long from Severn Tunnel East Box to Severn Tunnel West Box, and although this meant that a goods train might readily occupy the section for twenty minutes, that position had to be accepted. Many years later, after automatic colour-light signals controlled by track circuits had been thoroughly proved, the Severn Tunnel section was subdivided by a series of such signals and their use speeded up matters at times of heavy goods traffic. Everybody was delighted; all agreed that this was a great improvement.

There was, however, once a spot of bother that started with a burst boiler-water gauge and failure of the automatic shut-off valves to be automatic. This was on a passenger train heading slowly down inside the Tunnel in something like maximum murk with one at least of the men looking ahead for an automatic signal which they had to expect would be showing red and therefore ordering a stop right there. But however intent one may be on an important duty, a torrent of steam meeting a torrent of scalding water head-on at a point within a couple of feet of one's eyes forms an irresistible diversion. This fireman was diverted, and he and the driver took instant action to start coping with this murderous menace. They may not have taken long to do this, but by the time that they had sorted things out and peace reigned once more in the cab, both men suddenly realized that they didn't know whether they had passed the signal or not and so the only thing to do was to stop and then try to decide what to do next.

The fact that they could not see ahead of them the signal that the fireman had been looking for could mean either that they had passed it or that it was not far ahead but hidden by thick smoke. They had to guess which was the more likely. They eventually agreed that the fireman should go back along the track and find out whether they had passed the signal. So he lit one of their lamps and walked, between the train and the wall, back up the gradient in

163

search of a signal. There was an element of vagueness in his mission. How far should he go before deciding that they *couldn't* have passed it by all this much, and that it must be ahead of the engine? He might take the patient, thorough, self-righteous view that if he went on until he came to the end of the tunnel without coming across the signal, then it must be somewhere ahead of the engine. Apart from the primly virtuous characteristics of this view, it had the pleasant advantage that it demanded no judgment. You did not have to be continually asking yourself whether this is surely far enough to go; you had just to plod on mechanically until you came to daylight and then simply go to the signal-box and describe the position to the signalman before plunging back till you came to the engine again.

If on your way up you were to hear a train coming down the gradient by mistake you could warn the driver by sticking a detonator on a rail, except that as you did not originally think of walking all this way you did not bring any detonator with you. Pity! Still, as all the section is track-circuited no train is going to come down while the section is occupied.

When the fireman had been away from the footplate for some time, the driver began to form the opinion that this showed that they had not over-run the signal by any short distance and therefore that they had probably not over-run it at all. If that were the case the signal was ahead, not very far away, but obscured by smoke. Why not get down and find it and then whistle the fireman back? So the driver lit another lamp, got down on the floor and made his way ahead. He was surprised that he could still see no signal after going fifty or more yards ahead, but he kept going for a time and then stopped for further reflection. In what should have been a silence he was disturbed to hear a faint rumble behind him and had the horrifying thought that a train was coming down behind his own train. A few seconds later he realized that the sound he had heard was not that of a distant train going fairly fast, but that of his own train going fairly slowly. Before he had quite believed this, the engine was passing him, fairly slowly indeed but not slowly enough to enable him to size up the situation and try to get on to it – not that this would have been easy even in daylight, let alone in this murk. As the tender went past him, then the first coach, and then the second, he realized that here was a new situation that would bear thinking about. No immediate thought brought him any solace. He had left his engine unattended while attached to a train-load of passengers on a steep gradient over a mile from the bottom of the Severn Tunnel and now, unless the guard had noticed anything unusual (and what *could* he have noticed?) the train was going to run down to the bottom and some way up the other side, unless indeed it hit another train on the way!

Then if the road were clear it would start to run back to the bottom and up the gradient towards him. It would not come up to the position where he had left it standing, but if he could work out how far it might come, and if he knew where he was at the moment, he might with a bit of luck be near the engine where it stopped and would have a chance of getting on it and taking charge once more. With a bit of luck and everyone persuaded to keep his mouth shut, he might get out of this without any boss getting to know.

But then another dreadful thought came to him. So long as the driverless train was running in the right direction for the line it was on, the automatic signalling would stop any train (whose driver could see the signals!) from overtaking it, but after it had started to run in the wrong direction it could collide with any following train that had stopped at a signal. So there was no question of hiding anything. Any following train must be stopped as soon as it could be done and the only way of doing that was to warn the signalmen by breaking the tell-tale wire. So he did this and in case it was too late to have stopped some following train from passing the signal-box, the best he could do in his own interest was to get away from the probable point of collision. This meant that he had to get ahead of the signal that he still had not found.

So he pushed on ahead and at length found the signal showing red. This was naturally a great relief but even as he looked he got another violent shock as it changed to yellow! Any train that chanced along now would continue down the grade and, whether it stopped at the bottom or not, there would be a collision between it and the driverless train on its way back.

It might be possible to think of a more horrifying situation but this was bad enough. If there was a following train in the tunnel a collision was inevitable. Where it would occur it was impossible for anyone to predict. Where he should go to have the best chance of keeping out of it, neither he nor anyone else could say. His only firm policy was to listen for any approaching train, get into a refuge and hope for the best. The longer the time that elapsed before he heard a train the better, because the less the likelihood that it was approaching the runaway.

With no immediate notion as to which way was better to go, he stood in a refuge and thought a bit more about the position. Assuming that, as now seemed likely, the breaking of the wire had enabled the signalman to ensure that no other train would enter the tunnel until everything had been sorted out, what was going to happen? The train that he now hardly dare think of as 'his' would run for half a mile or so up the gradient, would then run back towards him and might indeed reach him and pass him. If it did pass him, not going very fast and of course slowing down pretty quickly, he might run after it and be lucky enough to reach the cab steps just before it stopped. If he could get back on the engine, he could stop the train and then have time to breathe, at least to the extent that anyone *could* breathe in all this smoke. Then it would be a matter of waiting for the fireman. It might take him some time to reach the engine if he had gone all the way to the signal-box, but at least it would be only a matter of time. Only, indeed! The delay would be at least half an hour and a great deal of explaining would have to be done. It looked as if no passenger was going to be hurt and no material damage done, but one driver was going to be severely censured. And even this was based on wishful thinking, because the chance of his being able to hop on to the engine next time it came anywhere near him was really remote. As he did not know how far he was from the place where the train had stopped, he had no idea whether the train would come right back to him or not. If it did, it might shoot past him too fast for him to think of joining it there or of catching it where it was going slowly enough. As he could form no idea whether it was better to go up or down, he might as well stop where he was till something happened.

Then he heard a rumble. As it strengthened he remained safe in his refuge and at length his train appeared, going back to where it had come from at a speed that discouraged any idea of following it on foot.

He argued that it would be going nearly as fast when it came back and began to wonder whether he might not stay where he was till it came up next time. It would not come up so far as it had this time and indeed it might not reach his present position. So he waited for it to run down past him again and then he followed on faltering feet. How far should he go? He just could not guess, and he thought that he might go right to the bottom where it would eventually stop.

Eventually, yes, but what might happen to the engine in the meantime? Would the water in the boiler get down to a dangerously low level and cause the fusible plugs to go? Or had the injector been working when he left the engine, in which case it would fill the boiler up to the whistle? Then the injector would stop and the boiler would start to blow off through the injector overflow and the water level would come down quickly and the plugs would go just the same.

He didn't think he'd left an injector working, but then neither did he think he'd left the small vacuum ejector working, and yet he must have done, as that was all that could have released the brakes.

And what was the guard doing all this time? He must have noticed that the train had stopped and started three times, but was he not even sufficiently interested to find out which way it was going? And if he did notice that something odd was going on, could he possibly guess what it was? And if he did, what would he do? He could stop the train at any time but what time and place would he choose? You would think he would put the brakes on when the train stopped itself, as he would think it strange that it should do so with its brakes off. If he did sort things out as well as that, would he decide to hold the train when it stopped with the engine pointing uphill? The driver hoped he would, because that would put the greatest depth of water over the firebox.

If the guard did that, would he think to get on to the engine and see where the water was? Would he know what to do if it were low? Or if he suspected that the water might be low, dare he go near the engine at all?

And when the driver himself eventually got near the engine, dare *he* get on to it? What a mess he was in! With that small ejector still working and dropping the water level by using steam, it was now not just a matter of delay or inconvenience – there could be serious danger if neither he nor the fireman could get to the engine pretty quickly.

He was tramping disconsolately and apprehensively down towards the bottom of the tunnel without knowing whether it was the right thing to do or not, when suddenly he heard ahead a rumble, which suggested that his faithful train was coming back to him again. He felt pretty sure by now that the message of the broken tell-tale wire was keeping the tunnel clear of any following train so that the risk of collision had vanished. He therefore stood against the wall and waited for the wheels to start passing him, so that he might judge whether there was any chance of getting on the engine this time. He put his lamp on the ground because of course he would need two free hands if he were to have any chance of pulling himself up, but as he watched wheels passing him he realized that it was quite impossible for him to get on unless the engine happened to stop just where he was, and even then it was risky in the limited light of the lamp.

No! the train and the engine went past him again without offering a chance of useful contact and without offering any encouragement to chase it. Might as well wait here as anywhere! Might just as well wait on the chance that next time it might stop here. But keep out of the way, she'll be coming back any minute now.

He waited for a minute or two but heard no returning rumble. Surely she should be coming back by now? Or had the guard stopped her? He started walking back up the gradient with something like the first glimmering of hope in his breast. As he went he heard a faint sound that was not a rumble but something more like the singing of an injector. So he hurried more hopefully still and presently distinguished through the now much thinner smoke the glare of the coach lights on the side of the tunnel and a light on the floor. There she was, safely stopped, and someone had got an injector going. Thank God!

As he came to the engine someone with a lamp came towards him from the side of the train. It was his fireman. Reunited at last, they got on to the footplate and found the boiler water nicely in sight.

The fireman put the handbrake on, as the driver ought to have done before he left. The driver turned off the small ejector which should never have been left on and started the big ejector to take the brakes off in the normal way.

The fireman related that after leaving the engine he had walked a long way back until he was absolutely convinced that they had not passed the signal and then retraced his steps down the bank towards the train. After what seemed a long walk he came to the signal, showing red, before he had seen any sign of the train. This he found odd because although he had admittedly been away from the engine for quite a long time the driver would surely not have gone on without him. Nevertheless he continued to walk on, and then rather suddenly saw the tail lamp of his train perhaps ten, perhaps twenty yards ahead. He continued to stride on but as he was getting no nearer he realized that the train was going away from him. He broke into a run and got a hand on the nearer buffer at the back of the last coach, but had to let it go.

He had been surprised not to find the train where he had left it, but was puzzled that it should start to run away when he had almost reached it. Again he found it hard to believe that the driver had gone on without him. To have done it once was rather funny. To do it twice was extraordinary. And then came the thought that the departure had not been very emphatic. He had not heard any exhaust sound. The gradient, and not the engine, had been allowed to start the train. It was then that he began to consider the possibility that the driver was not on the engine. If that was the case, the train would go down to the bottom, run some distance up the other side, come back and then repeat the cycle. Was that, in fact, what it had already done? Anyhow the right thing to do was to keep walking down and with a bit of luck he might just be there to catch the train at the end of its next back stroke and do something about stopping it.

It did in fact happen just like that, but this time he had worked out what to do. He would not try to get on to the engine. He would concern himself solely with the rear coach. So as it came towards him he ran alongside it till it had nearly stopped, then whipped round the back and with one relentless right-hander knocked the vacuum brake pipe off its dummy. The brakes went on with a bang that brought the guard to his platform-side window. The fireman told him to keep his handbrake on till he heard a whistle from the engine. The fireman then put the brake pipe back on its dummy and went ahead to the engine.

Aware of the risk that the boiler water was low with the engine standing on a steep down-grade, he climbed on to the footplate and without pausing to look at the water-gauge he started an injector, got off again quickly, and retreated alongside the train. After a few minutes the water fed into the boiler had removed whatever risk there had been of melting a plug and just as he was preparing to get up on the engine again he saw a light and behind it the driver coming out of the gloom.

By the time this story had been related the vacuum brakes were off and so the driver whistled to tell the guard that the engine had been re-manned and would he mind taking his handbrake off. They then resumed their interrupted journey with driver and guard mentally scribbling out cover stories. A sound story would have to cover the broken tell-tale wire and also the fact that one Nosey Parker of a passenger had reported to the guard that the train had passed over the bottom level bit of the tunnel four times up to then, and which way would the train go when the driver had made his mind up?

So it all had to come out and it led, amongst many other things, to the opinion that automatic signals in the Severn Tunnel were not an entirely good thing.

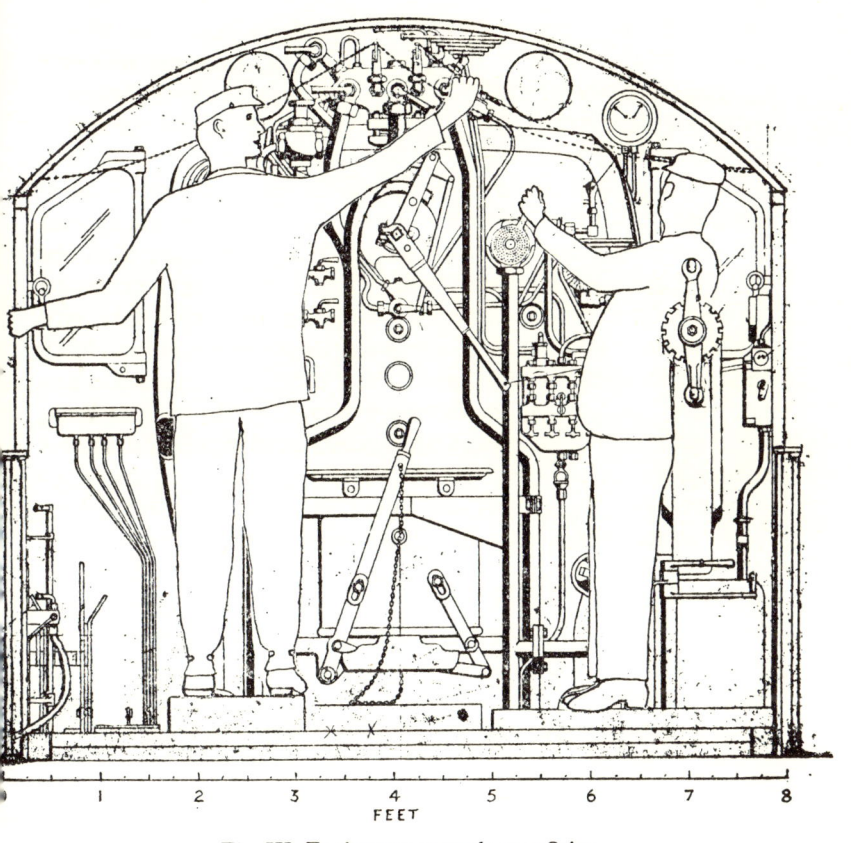

FEET

Fig. IX. Enginemen at work on a Saint

CHAPTER 11

Conclusion

⤜⤛

The writer of an article in the *Railway Magazine* in about 1926 mentioned that he had ridden from Euston to Crewe in the same compartment as a young man who made a list of the numbers of the locomotives he saw on the way. The writer of the article thought this was a most extraordinary thing to do, and so did I. Many years had to elapse before such listing of numbers became a popular pastime and even then it did not strike me as being worthwhile. I could not see why my seeing a particular locomotive should give it such distinction as to justify a special note of its number.

My own interests were far less in names and numbers than in locomotives themselves, in their form, in their mechanical details and in the ways of handling them. I once found great interests of these kinds in Great Western engine *Grosvenor* and this name I did remember although all I could have said about the number was that it probably had four figures.

Fifteen years later I found the Great Western engine of that name mentioned as having put up in her early days 'a good performance' by taking a train of about 200 tons from Bristol to Exeter, $75\frac{1}{2}$ miles, in 80 minutes start-to-stop. She averaged 72 m.p.h. over 13 miles or so from Tiverton Junction down to Cowley Bridge Junction. This was quite bright for a train in regular service at the end of the nineteenth century.

In the same article, *Earl Cawdor*, a locomotive of the same class as *Grosvenor*, was mentioned as having run a train of ten 8-wheel vehicles from London to Oxford at 55·9 m.p.h. average and thence to Birmingham at 57·2 m.p.h. Apparently unconvinced that this was brilliant, the writer of the article wrote that it was 'by no means poor work'.

Even though some locomotive might never have distinguished itself in power or speed, its identification by number or name was essential for practical reasons and agreeable for emotional ones.

How heart-warming it used to be to re-encounter a locomotive after a great interval in time and space!

I once saw an up train from Plymouth stop at Totnes with the engine No. 4096 *Highclere Castle* right at the platform ramp. When the rightaway was given, the fireman went down the ramp to the front of the engine and as she started slowly away he walked alongside her to find which of the inside-cylinder glands was making an audible blow.

Years later I was awakened on a brilliant Sunday morning at The Grove Hotel close to Walcot station in Shropshire by a roaring sound, which I found came from the safety valves of No. 4096 as she paused with a stopping train that left (I now find from Bradshaw for the summer of 1938) at 7.58 a.m. for Shrewsbury. This was a light easily-timed stopping train and for a Castle in charge of it to be blowing off after 8 miles of downhill and more to follow showed pretty poor enginemanship, but all the same I should be glad to think that I could go to Walcot and repeat the experience. (How many spotters would notice that 4096 is the twelfth power of 2?)

I also found from Bradshaw, although I do not remember noticing it on the spot, that a down train was booked to leave Walcot at the same time, 7.58 a.m. At Wellington this train stood for 7 minutes, possibly to allow for delays to the connecting train booked to arrive from Crewe at 8 a.m.

Just think of it! Even on *Sunday* mornings one could leave Crewe by Great Western train at 6.45 a.m. and travel through gentle countryside to Wellington with stops at Nantwich, Audlem, Market Drayton, Tern Hill, Hodnet, Peplow and Crudgington, but not at Adderley. And as if this string of rural names were not enough, there were halts at Coole Pilate, Coxbank, Little Drayton, Wollerton, Ellerdine and Rowton – names to excite the imagination even of those who do not know that all around is verdant peace with the great arc of the Wrekin dominating the southern horizon.

This was no speedway, the booked average from Crewe to Wellington being between 25 and 26 m.p.h., but who would want to rush through such country at that time on a sunny morning behind a double-frame Duke? What delight can the sere and dark-yellow pages of Bradshaw recreate!

And what mystery too! As the 6.45 from Crewe rolled into Wellington at 8.00 a.m., another train was booked to go back along its route as far as Crudgington, to arrive at 8.09 a.m. and to go no farther. At that point, so far as Bradshaw revealed, this train ceased to exist; no corresponding return train to Wellington was shown.

How pleased one would be if things had had such permanence, that one might go to Wellington or Crudgington on some clement spring Sunday to see what did happen to the 8.00 a.m. down the branch!

The Great Western had many rural branches in beautiful country, but just think of such a branch leading Great Western trains to Crewe! It brought a variety of Great Western locomotives into that North Western stronghold and very different they looked in their green and brass from Crewe engines in shining black and later in LMS red. This changed with the years and once in the late 1940s I heard a young spotter on the footbridge at Crewe exclaim 'What a wreck!' when a neglected, unkempt Great Western 2/2-6-0 went through to the North shed to be turned.

Before the 1923 grouping dirty engines were hardly ever seen (before 1916 they were never seen) and the Dukes that used to work the passenger trains between Wellington and Crewe merged gleamingly with the green landscape. Not all Great Western landscapes were green, but the exceptions were well outnumbered. A commuter between (say) Wednesbury and Snow Hill in Birmingham could concentrate on his newspaper without missing anything very stimulating from outside the train, and a commuter between Ealing and Paddington might think himself not much better off in this respect. Neither of them would naturally think of the Great Western as a scenic line, but an onlooker may be excused for taking a broader view. The enthusiastic student of Great Western steam in action is justified in thinking of it in purely rural surroundings, because that was where most Great Western mileage lay.

Between Reading and Taunton the Limited and the Torbay ran for 106 miles without passing a town of any size and the enchanted traveller might well imagine that the gentle scenery had been created for the Great Western to run through, although he might also discern a sharp incongruity between the colourful serenity of the countryside and the toil of the fireman in coal dust, heat and draught.

Coal itself could dominate views more exciting than meadows to Great Western directors. Before World War I export of coal was an operation in which the Great Western participated and the acres of coal visible in trains of railway wagons in sidings near the staiths beckoned good business for the Great Western. In every age there are those to whom the most beautiful word in the English language is 'cash' and that was what coal meant to Great Western shareholders. It did so in one way that now seems rather remarkable, and that was the transport of Welsh coal from Pontypool Road to Birkenhead. That long haul up the Welsh border took coal trains through the General Station at Shrewsbury; it was one of a number of features of diverse interest in the working of that small but very busy station.

The Great Western played a large part (perhaps the major part) in railway operations there and it was one of the most interesting places in Great Britain for the observer of locomotives and trains. Shrewsbury itself, by now almost destroyed by Development, is a town built on a hill within an extraordinary convolution of the River Severn, the station spanning the river between the castle and the county gaol. None of this used to be easily visible when the station had an extensive roof, nor could one see any more of it from the old footbridge which was heavily timbered and roofed save where frosted glass admitted some daylight.

Some of the markedly inefficient features of the steam locomotive contributed most to its emotional appeal and the interest of Shrewsbury for the locomotive enthusiast was intensified by what was, viewed from any broadly rational standpoint, operational inefficiency. This was engine-changing on trains that were passing at Shrewsbury from Great Western to North Western haulage, or the opposite.

Every north-to-west train (from Liverpool and Manchester to

Pontypool Road and beyond) had been 'pieced up' or reshuffled at Crewe, 34 miles back, and at Shrewsbury its North Western (or LMS) engine was replaced by a Great Western engine. The North Western engine might be a Precursor or an Experiment, and the LMS engine could be a Crewe Pacific that would spend some hours idle at Shrewsbury, return to Crewe with a train, and spend more idle hours there before taking a train to Glasgow or Perth. Or a North Western or LMS engine might similarly spend some restful time at Shrewsbury as part of its very first passenger-train job after being built or after major repairs at Crewe.

So at Shrewsbury, in a scene of Great Western activity one might see the very latest come from Crewe and leave a train that changed engines twice in 35 miles. In a properly integrated railway system there would be no engine-changing in any train journey shorter than about 250 miles.

At Shrewsbury one could readily distinguish the different degrees of zip that could be applied to the elementary operation of detaching an engine from a train and moving it out of the way. At Shrewsbury one would form the impression that in this respect Great Western men were smarter than the other lot. Perhaps they were, but this was no evidence of it. Great Western men leaving north-bound trains were usually ending a turn of duty. North Western or LMS men leaving south-bound trains were usually not.

The urge to get home quickly outweighed a facility in those LMS locomotives with steam brakes. This was that the driver could release the engine's brakes immediately the train had stopped, whereas vacuum brakes on the engine could not be released until the fireman had separated the brake pipes between the tender and the train and had placed the pipe behind the tender on its dummy. The driver of a steam-braked engine could have reversed it and made it compress the buffers to take the load off the coupling before the fireman had transferred a lamp from the front of the engine to the back of the tender.

On the whole they were pretty deliberate at Shrewsbury and when, as happened at intervals throughout the day, trains came in bunches, most of them were delayed, first by being stopped and held before entering the station and secondly by failure of the plat-

14a. Two miles a minute in 1906.

b. Two million miles before 1954.

form staff to have completed their work even in the time occupied by engine changing. The only kind of credit that Shrewsbury commonly got for its traffic handling was the opinion that things were worse at Hereford. Imperfections of this kind did not worry the trainwatcher; on the contrary, they enabled him to see the trains for longer periods.

Train watching was not a basically clean operation and after an hour or two one might wonder where one could wash. I once addressed this question to one of the staff at Shrewsbury and was told that there were no facilities on the station, but that one could wash on a train. Only at the moment of writing this has it occurred to me that he may have imagined me to have been on the station with the purpose of joining a train. But although this was not the case, I saw nothing unreasonable in his remarks and every time I washed myself on Shrewsbury station after that it was in a through train during its station time. If one entered the train for the purpose as soon as it stopped, there was no need to hurry.

But to revert to purely Great Western matters at Shrewsbury I may refer to something that impressed me at the time as being successively remarkable, astonishing and amusing. From one of the other platforms I had seen a Great Western train run alongside the outer up platform at about 40 m.p.h. (at least twice as fast as was usual there) as if not to stop at Shrewsbury which would have been very remarkable. But then came a strong grinding of brakes, and to my astonishment the train stopped at the usual place. To my further astonishment after I had reached the engine with the hope of finding what all this meant I found the rear of the tender accurately stopped at the water column and they were taking water as usual. I could not refrain from asking the driver whether he could do that every time he wanted. He did not answer my question directly, but said, obviously seething, 'We've been stuck outside for thirteen bloody minutes.'

Few incidents were so stimulating as that, and most engine changing was so placidly matter-of-fact that I might make something out of one by noticing that the number of the Great Western engine was twice the number of the year of my birth and that the number of the North Western engine was as near as it could be to one thousand divided by the square root of two. No one could have suspected how the second number would dominate a particular field of transport over thirty years later.

I learned a little of aerodynamics from an observation on a Saint that had reached the station after passing through a rainstorm at full speed. On the table in front of the smokebox saddle raindrops lay in straight lines symmetrically convergent back from the buffer beam and one was bound to wonder why. What made the air that was deflected by the buffer beam move towards the centre-line of the locomotive? The answer could be only that it wasn't doing that. Air does not move on convergent paths unless it is being forced between convergent guides.

No! the rain-drop lines were made by air coming *forward* after having been struck by the smokebox door and deflected downwards. It then moved forwards and outwards, and on reaching the buffer beam was deflected upwards and backwards, forming a cylindrical vortex 8 ft wide.

Shrewsbury was perhaps unique in that one could see there regular trains of every description and the oldest and newest locomotives of two of the three largest railways in Britain. It must be added that only for a short period did the Great Western Kings work regularly into Shrewsbury. They were employed for a time on North to West trains but, so it is said, they caused, or were suspected to have caused, trouble with the track in certain places and so the experiment was discontinued. But this was no great hardship as Castles could handle the traffic satisfactorily.

A notable duty undertaken by Saints, Stars and Castles in successively later periods was a through engine-working between Shrewsbury and Newton Abbot, some 216 miles. This was a run of varied railway geography, but except between Pontypool Road and Bristol, where industry dimmed the prospect in places, the scenery was beautiful in a range of different ways and both start and finish were in pleasant small towns. One would like to think that the enginemen were usually so well on top of the job as to be able to appreciate this, although with summits at Church Stretton, Llanvihangel and Whiteball to think about and the Severn Tunnel trough to get through this was no easy road.

World War II brought greater variety than ever in the locomotives seen at Shrewsbury. Among the regular Great Western new-

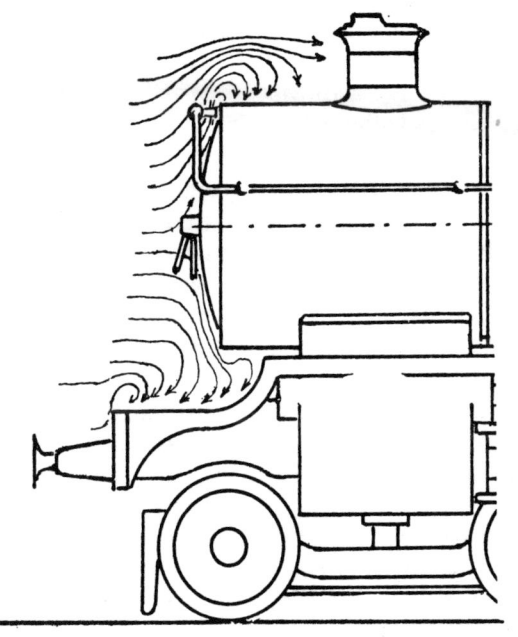

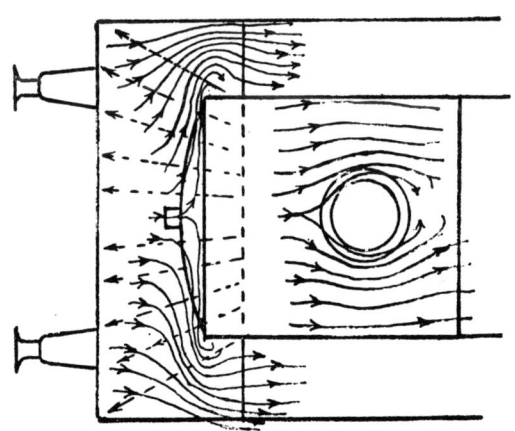

Fig. X. Air currents at the front of a Saint

179

comers were 5600 class 0–6–2Ts, 4200 class 2/2–8–0Ts and 7200 class 2/2–8–2Ts, which rarely, if ever, had worked to Shrewsbury before the war.

After the war, and after nationalization of the railways, and with the gradual reduction of railway traffic the story of Shrewsbury and indeed of all ex Great-Western work gradually lost its glamour and sickened. Steam has gone and even unskilled hands can do what work there is with expensive diesel locomotives, twice as big as should suffice for the job. In these men may commit suicide by going to sleep as they run, proving the uselessness of devices intended to save them and their passengers. The term 'dead man's handle' has won a new significance. Air-braked goods trains come to grief because no one has bothered to connect the pipes and as the guard rides on the engine there is no one but the driver to find whether the brakes are working or not.

The fifty-year-old driver of an express train from Paddington to Bristol *didn't know* that the relief line ended beyond Didcot and that there was therefore a swerve to the left just past that station for trains on the down relief. The signals didn't warn him as they showed a succession of green lights. The track layout didn't warn him as it presented a dead straight run on to the *up* relief line from Steventon. The driver didn't know, wasn't told and couldn't guess about the swerve until he saw the point blades and then there was no time for him to do anything to diminish the immediate danger. Contrary to any reasonable expectation, the locomotive and some of the vehicles remained on the rails but others slid along in unscheduled attitudes till the brakes brought everything to rest.

Then at Hixon . . . but need we go on? Who would want to? It's enough to have been caught up in a permissive society without re-examining its horrors. It's much more pleasant to look farther back. On page 160A are pictures of the most distinguished Lady and the last Saint to survive. Look at the Lady and remember how in 1906 those reckless men pressed her into indiscreet energy on Hullavington bank. Or was it the Lady herself who made the running by pulling the pole out of the driver's control? But remember also the prodigies of solid work that she and her sisters did for thirty years afterwards.

Look at *Saint David* and think of two million miles of hard and fast service. Remember that Saint-style locomotives dominated the Great Western main-line scene from Edwardian days right to the end of steam. The Churchward Saints did more than open a new era; they went on to end it. Their pictures deserve long looks.

Admire the comfortable set of the boiler between the splashers, the mighty cylinder, the grand sweep of the connecting rod across one-and-a-half wheels and the proud projection of the smokebox, eager to go.

This was a design, strong in simplicity, that over sixty years ago brought the steam locomotive to its highest economic refinement and one may be thrilled to recognize this in the very line and structure of the Churchward Saint. The reader who cannot see this need not despair; life is not limited to locomotives. But he is missing something that is a permanent joy to more fortunate observers.

TABLES

The figures in this table are intended to give some details about the engines of certain Great Western classes. The tables are a concentration of published information which is not all self-consistent even where it is official. The figures quoted cannot be claimed to be more than approximate. The constantly changing dimensions of every individual locomotive is in itself enough to prohibit accuracy, and the full story would demand a book as big as this for each and every one of the 3000-odd Great Western locomotives.

In some cases, for example that of w27, the running numbers of the engines of a class can be concisely displayed and this is done. In difficult cases displayed information is limited to the smallest and largest numbers with an intervening x to show that all the other engine numbers lay between them.

Renumbering of engines delighted some historians and infuriated others. An extensive one was done in 1913 to place all the Bulldogs and Birds in one series extending from 3300 to 3455. Another decision, was that the 2700s, for example, should extend from 2700 to 2799 rather than from 2701 to 2800, which had been the original choice.

TABLE I

Reference	W1	W2	W4	W6	W7	W10	W11	W12	W15
Engineer	G	G	G	G	P	G	G	G	G
Wheel arrangement	222	222	222	422	424 WT	440 ST	440 ST	440	2/240 T
Class	Star	Firefly	Great Western	Iron Duke	B&E	Corsair	Sappho	Waverley	Metro
Number built	12	62	1	29	8	2	13	10	22
Date of first	1837	1840	1846	1847	1853	1849	1854	1855	1862
Date of last	1841	1842	1846	1855	1854	1849	1855	1855	1864
Grate area (sq. ft)	13·6	13·5	22·6	21·7	23	19	18·5	19·2	18·0
Barrel diam. (ins)	48	48	48	58	48	51	54	54	57
Barrel length (ins)	102	102	126	132	129	126	126	132	126
Heating surface									
Firebox (sq. ft)	70	97	151	148	150	121	121	130	?
Tubes (sq. ft)	655	602	1582	1800	900	1134	1134	1444	?
NTE* (1000 lbs)	2·5	2·1	7	7	?	9	9	7	9
Adhesive wt (ton)	8	10	12	13	19	21	24	22	?
Engine (ton)	18	24	29	36	42	36	39	37	?
Tender (ton)	?	?	?	17	?	?	?	26	—
Boiler pressure† (p.s.i.)	60	50	100	100	?	100	100	100	120
Cylinder diam. (ins)	16	15	18	18	16½	17	17	17	16
Piston stroke (ins)	16	18	24	24	24	24	24	24	24
Wheel diam. (ins)	84	84	96	96	108	72	69	84	72
Valve type and pos.	F2	F2	F2	F2	F2	F2	F2	F2	F2
Valve gear	A	A	A	G	S	G	G	G	G
Description p.	30	—	32	33	41	36	36	35	38
Illustration p.	—	—	59	60	32A	57	—	60	—
Running Nos.	—	—	—	—	39–46	—	—	—	—

Line 0   G – Gooch   P – Pearson
Line 21   Flat valves between cylinders
Line 22   A – Gab motion   G – Gooch gear   S – Stephenson gear
All broad-gauge engines

* Nominal tractive effort at 85 per cent of maximum boiler pressure
† Maximum pressure permitted by setting of safety valves

TABLE I *cont.*

	Reference	W20	W22	W23	W24	W27	W30	W31	W34	W35
0	Engineer	G	G	AJ	AJ	D	D	D	D	D
1	Wheel arrangement	060	060ST	060T	222	222	240	240	440	440
2	Class	Caesar	Bank-ing	*Sir Watkin*	*Sir Daniel*	3001 ..	3201 Stella	3206 Bar-num	— Arm-strong	3252 Duke
3	Number built	8	4	6	30	30	20	20	4	59
4	Date of first	1851	1852	1865	1866	1891	1884	1889	1894	1895
5	Date of last	1852	1854	1866	1869	1892	1885	1889	1894	1899
6	Grate area (sq. ft)	18·4	19·2	20·8	16·6	20·8	15·2	19·0	2·08	19·0
7	Barrel diam. (ins)	51	54	53	50	51	53	51	51	53
8	Barrel length (ins)	126	132	132	132	138	123	132	138	132
9	Heating surface									
10	Firebox (sq. ft)	121	128	112	98	124	103	116	127	113
11	Tubes (sq. ft)	1134	1290	1220	1105	1343	1107	1353	1434	1286
12										
13	NTE (1000 lbs)	11	12	14	10	15	15	14	17	18
14	Adhesive wt (ton)	28	38	41	13	19	26	29	32	29
15	Engine wt (ton)	28	38	41	30	45	36	43	51	46
16	Tender wt (ton)	?	—	—	24	33	33	33	37	24
17	Boiler pressure (p.s.i.)	120	120	120	140	160	140	150	160	165
18	Cylinder diam. (ins)	16	17	17	17	20	17	18	20	18
19	Piston stroke (ins)	24	24	24	24	24	26	24	26	26
20	Wheel diam. (ins)	60	60	54	84	92½	61	73½	85½	68
21	Valve type and pos.	F2	F2	F2	F2	F3	F2	F3	F3	F3
22	Valve gear	G	G	S	S	S	S	S	S	S
23	Description p.	—	—	—	—	46	48	—	49	50
24	Illustration p.	32B	58	—						
25	Running Nos.	—	—		378 ×586	3001 −30	3201 −05 3501 −20	3206 −25	4169 −72	32 − 33 −

Line o   AJ – James Armstrong   D – Dean   G – Gooch

Line 21   F2 –Flat valves between cylinders
                 F3 – Flat valves below cylinders

Line 22   S – Stephenson   G-Gooch

Items W20 W22 W23 were broad-gauge engines

TABLE I cont.

(Running numbers in brackets were altered in 1913)

Reference	W36	W37	W38	W40	W41	W42	W43	W44	W48
Engineer	D	D	D	D	D	D	D	Ch	Ch
Wheel arrangement	440	440	440	440	440	440	440	440	440
No. of first	(3292)	(3312)	(3310)	3553	3528	(3353)	(3373)	(3405)	(3731)
Class	4100	3311	4118	3553	3528	3341	4120	3700	3441
Class name	Bad-minton	Bull-dog	Water-ford	3521	3521	Bull-dog	Atbara	City	Bird
Number built	19	40	1	26	14	40	29	20	15
Date of first	1897	1898	1899	1899	1900	1900	1900	1902	1909
Date of last	1899	1898	1899	1900	1902	1903	1901	1903	1910
Grate area (sq. ft)	18·3	23·5	23·5	17·2	21·4	21·5	21·3	20·6	20·4
Barrel diam. (ins)	53	55	55	51	54	54	54	66	61
Barrel length (ins)	132	132	132	123	123	132	132	132	132
Heating surface									
Firebox (sq. ft)	122	124	124	110	125	125	124	128	121
Tubes (sq. ft)	1175	1396	1396	1070	1437	1540	1540	1818	1397
NTE (1000 lbs)	16	19	16	15	18	19	16	18	21
Adhesive wt (ton)	33	32	34	38	32	33	34	36	35
Engine wt (ton)	53	50	52	42	46	50	52	56	52
Tender wt (ton)	33	33	33	35	35	35	33	37	37
Boiler pres. (p.s.i.)	180	180	180	150	180	180	180	195	200
Cylinder diam. (ins)	18	18	18	17	17	18	18	18	18
Piston stroke (ins)	26	26	26	24	24	26	26	26	26
Wheel diam. (ins)	80½	68	80½	62	62	68	80½	80½	68
Valve type and pos.	F3	F3	F3	F2	F2	F3	F3	F3	F3
Valve gear	S	S	S	S	S	S	S	S	S
Description p.	50	64	64	—	—	—	—	—	—
Illustration p.	—	80A	80A	64A	64A	—	—	—	144B
Running Nos.	(3292 × 3311)	3300– 39	4118	3521 × 3560	3524 × 3559	3341– 80	4120– 48	3700– 19	3441– 55
Dome	Yes	Yes	No	Yes	No	No	No	No	No
Firebox	HB	HB	HB	B	HB	HB	HB	BT	BT
Smokebox	L	E	E	N	ES	ES	ES	ES	ES
Frame	C	C	C	S	S	S	S	S	D

Line 0   Ch – Churchward   D – Dean   W40/41 were rebuilds of W53
Line 21   F2 – Flat valves between cylinders
          F3 – Flat valves below cylinders
          Some W43 had 6½-in. piston valves below cylinders
Line 27   B – Belpaire   BT – Belpaire with taper barrel
          HB – Belpaire markedly higher than barrel
Line 28   E – Extended   L – long extension
          N – wrapper type, normal length   S – on saddle
Line 29   C – top edge with curves   D – deep with straight top edge
          S – top edge straight   All were double frames

TABLE I *cont.*

Reference	W51	W53	W55	W57	W59	W60	W62	W6
0 Engineer	AJ	D	D	Co	AJ	AJ	D	D
1 Wheel arrangement	240T	042T	242T	042T	060	060	060	06
1A Frame	S/SO	D	S	SO	D	D	S	D
2 Class	455	3521	3600	4800	322	388	2301	236
2A Class name	Metro	—	—	—	Beyer	Std gds	Dean gds	
3 Number built	140	40	31	95	30	240	260	2
4 Date of first	1869	1887	1900	1932	1864	1866	1883	188
5 Date of last	1899	1889	1903	1936	1866	1876	1899	188
6 Grate area (sq. ft)	15·8	18·9	21·4	12·8	15·8	16·6	16·4	15·
7 Barrel diam. (ins)	49	51	54	46	48	50	51	5
8 Barrel length (ins)	126	123	123	120	146	132	123	12
9 Heating surface								
10 Firebox (sq. ft)	92	125	125	83	108	98	114	10
11 Tubes (sq. ft)	1116	1070	1437	870	1132	1105	1080	109
12								
13 NTE (1000 lbs)	13	18	14	14	14	14	14	1
14 Adhesive wt (ton)	25	33	35	28	32	31	37	3
15 Engine wt (ton)	34	48	65	42	32	31	37	3
16 Tender wt (ton)					26	26	34	3
17 Boiler pres. (p.s.i.)	140	180	140	165	140	140	140	14
18 Cylinder diam. (ins)	16	17	17	16	17	17	17	1
19 Piston stroke (ins)	24	24	24	24	24	24	24	2
20 Wheel diam. (ins)	60	60	62	62	60	60	62	6
21 Valve type and pos.	F2	F2	6½P1/3	F2	F2	F2	F2	F2
22 Valve gear	S	S	S	S	S	S	S	S
23 Description p.	—	—	68	—	—	—	—	—
24 Illustration p.	48A	48B	48B	48A	32B	32B	—	—
25 Running Nos.	455× 3599	3521– 60	3600– 30	4800– 74 5800– 19	322× 359	21× 1215	2301– 60 2381– 2580	2361 80

Line 0   AJ – James Armstrong   Co–Collett   D– Dean

Line 1A   D – Double   S – Single   SO – Single, but with outside axleboxes fo: the uncoupled axle

Line 21   F2 – Flat valves between cylinders

6½P1/3 – 6½-in. piston valves, one above and between cylinders, the ot! below

W53 were rebuilt to W40 or W41

TABLE I *cont.*

	Reference	W67	W71	W81	W84	W86	W88	W89	W90	W91
o	Engineer	AJ	D	H	Ch	Co	Co	Co	Co	H
1	Wheel arrangement	060ST	060ST	060PT	2/460	4/460	2/460	2/460	2/460	2/460
2	Class	1076	1661	9400	2900	4073	4900	6800	7800	1000
A	Class name				Saint	Castle	Hall	Grange	Manor	County
3	Number built	325	40	210	77	155	330	80	30	30
4	Date of first	1870	1886	1947	1903	1923	1928	1936	1938	1945
5	Date of last	1881	1887	1956	1913	1950	1950	1939	1950	1947
6	Grate area (sq. ft)	16·9	15·2	17·4	27·1	29·4	27·1	27·1	22·1	28·8
A	Standard boiler No.			10	1	8	1	1	14	15
7	Barrel diam. (ins)	50	53	60	66	69	66	66	63	69
8	Barrel length (ins)	132	126	123	178	178	178	178	150	152
9	Heating surface									
o	Firebox (sq. ft)	98	103	102	155	163	155	155	140	169
1	Tubes (sq. ft)	1062	1054	1070	1687	1858	1687	1687	1286	1545
2	Superheater (sq. ft)			74	263	263	263	263	182	265
3	NTE (1000 lbs)	16	15	23	25	32	28	29	28	33
4	Adhesive wt (ton)	38	46	56	55	59	57	56	51	59
5	Engine wt (ton)	38	46	56	72	80	75	74	69	77
6	Tender wt (ton)				40	40/47	47	40	40	49
7	Boiler pressure (p.s.i.)	140	140	200	225	225	225	225	225	280
8	Cylinder diam. (ins)	17	17	17½	18½	16	18½	18½	18	18½
9	Piston stroke (ins)	24	26	24	30	26	30	30	30	30
o	Wheel diam. (ins)	54	60	55½	80½	80½	72	72	68	75
1	Valve type and pos.	F2	F2	F2	10P1	8P1	10P1	10P1	10P1	10P1
2	Valve gear	S	S	S	S	WR	S	S	S	S
3	Description p.	—	48	—	92	—	108	109	110	111
4	Illustration p.	48B	—	58	160A	—	96B	96B	96B	144A
5	Running Nos.	727	1661	3400	2900	111	4900	6800	7800	1000
		×	–	×	×	×	×	–	–	–
		1660	1700	9499	2998	7037	7929	79	29	29

Line o   AJ – James Armstrong   Co – Collett   Ch – Churchward
           H – Hawksworth
Line 21   F2 – Flat valves between cylinders
           10P1 – 10-in. piston valves above cylinders
           8P1 – 8-in. piston valves above cylinders
Line 22   S – Stephenson   WR – Walschaerts with rocking levers for outside valves

TABLE I *cont.*

Reference		W95	W96	W101	W103	W107	W109	W110	W112
0	Engineer	Ch	Ch	Ch	Co	Ch	D	Ch	Ch
1	Wheel arrangement	2/262T	2/260	2/280T	2/282T	2/442	440PT	2/440	2/442
2	Class	4500	4300	4200	7200	171	1490	3800	4600
2A	Class name					Atlantic		County	
3	Number built	175	342	205	54	14	1	40	
4	Date of first	1906	1911	1910	1934	1905	1898	1904	1913
5	Date of last	1929	1932	1940	1939	1905	1898	1912	1913
6	Grate area (sq. ft)	16·6	20·6	20·6	20·6	27·1	20·4	20·6	16·6
6A	Standard boiler No.	5	4	4	4	1		4	5
7	Barrel diam. (ins)	57	66	66	66	66	55	66	57
8	Barrel length (ins)	126	132	132	132	178	128	132	126
9	Heating surface								
10	Firebox (sq. ft)	96	122	129	129	155	93	129	94
11	Tubes (sq. ft)	1177	1228	1350	1350	1990	1392	1350	1178
12	Superheater (sq. ft)		216	192	192			192	
13	NTE (1000 lbs)	20	26	32	34	25	16	21	18
14	Adhesive wt (ton)	44	53	72	73	39	35	38	31
15	Engine wt (ton)	57	62	82	93	71	51	59	61
16	Tender wt (ton)		40			40		40	
17	Boiler pres. (p.s.i.)	180	200	200	200	225	165	200	200
18	Cylinder (ins)	17	18½	18½	19	18½	15½	18	17
19	Piston stroke (ins)	24	30	30	30	30	26	30	24
20	Wheel diam. (ins)	55½	68	55½	55½	80½	55½	80½	68
21	Valve type and pos.	8P1	10P1	10P1	10P1	10P1	F2	10P1	8P1
22	Valve gear	S	S	S	S	S	S	S	S
23	Description p.	—	72	—	—	88	67	—	—
24	Illustration p.	80B	144A	144A	144A	96A	72	96A	80F
25	Running Nos.	4500–99 5500–74	4300× 9319	4200–99 5200–94	7200–53	171–2 179–190	1490	3800–39	4600

Line 0   Ch – Churchward   Co – Collett   D – Dean
Line 21   F2 – Flat valves between cylinders
              P1 – 8-in. or 10-in. valves above cylinders
Line 22   S – Stephenson valve gear
              W101 – Ten of these were given numbers 5255–5264 that had been used on
              similar engines before conversion to W103 and re-numbering
              W103 – Rebuilds of W101

TABLE I *cont.*

	Reference	W113	W114	W115	W116	W117	W118	W119	W120
o	Engineer	D	D	D	D	Ch	Ch	Ch	Ch
1	Wheel arrangement	460	460	260	260	260	4/462	262T	2/060ST
2	Class	36	2601	2602	33	2662	111	3901	1361
2A	Class name		Kruger	Mrs K	A'dare	A'dare	Gt Bear		
3	Number built	1	1	9	62	19	1	20	5
4	Date of first	1896	1899	1899	1900	1902	1908	1907	1910
5	Date of last	1896	1899	1903	1902	1907	1908	1910	1910
6	Grate area (sq. ft)	35·0	32	32	21·5	20·6	41·8	16·6	10·7
7	Barrel diam. (ins)	55	58	58	54	66	72	57	46
8	Barrel length (ins)	168	126	126	132	132	276	126	98
9	Heating surface								
10	Firebox (sq. ft)	116	169	169	125	128	158	94	75
11	Tubes (sq. ft)	1400	1713	1713	1538	1690	2700	1178	816
12	Superheater (sq. ft)						545		
13	NTE (1000 lbs)	25	28	28	24	26	28	21	15
14	Adhesive wt (ton)	48	52	52	48	50	60	48	35
15	Engine wt (ton)	60	64	61	56	57	97	63	35
16	Tender wt (ton)	36	33	37	37	37	46		
17	Boiler pres. (p.s.i.)	165	180	180	180	200	225	200	150
18	Cylinder diam. (ins)	20	19	19	18	18	15	17½	16
19	Piston stroke (ins)	24	28	28	26	26	26	24	20
20	Wheel diam. (ins)	54	55½	55½	55½	55½	80½	62	44
21	Valve type and pos.	F3	8½P1	8½P1	6½P3	F3	8P1	F2	F2
22	Valve gear	S	SR1	SR1	S	S	WR2	S	S
23	Description p.	65	65	65	66	66	—	—	—
24	Illustration p.	—	—	—	32B	—	—	48B	—
25	Running Nos.	36	2601	2602–10	2600–61	2662–80	111	3901–20	1361–5

Line o   Ch – Churchward   D – Dean

Line 21   F2 – Flat valves between cylinders   F3 – Flat valves below cylinders
         P1 – Piston valves above cylinders   P3 – Piston valves below cylinders
         Number is diameter of valve in inches

Line 22   S – Stephenson   R1 – Rocking shafts   R2 – Rocking arms
         W – Walschaerts

TABLE 2

Engine: 2949 *Stanford Court* (p. 106)
Load: 323 tons tare   340 tons full

Miles		Min.	sec.	Average m.p.h.	Local max. or min. m.p.h.
0·0	Cardiff	0	0	—	—
4·1	St Fagans	5	57	41·3	—
11·1	Llantrisant	13	20	56·8	—
13·6	Llanharan	16	05	54·5	52
20·2	Bridgend	22	05	66	60*
24·3	Stormy Siding	26	45	52·7	48
25·7	Pyle	28	03	64·6	—
29·7	Margam Moor	31	00	81·2	90
32·3	Port Talbot	33	15	69·3	63
37·9	Neath	38	45	61·2	30*
39·9	Skewen	42	25	32·7	30
44·5	Landore	48	20	46·8	—

* Speed restriction

TABLE 3

Trip by Saint class 2/4–6–0 No. 2922 *Saint Gabriel* (p. 145–162)
14/12/10/8 vehicles to Westbury/Taunton/Exeter/Plymouth
530/455/385/310 tons loaded

Miles		Sched. Time (min.)	Actual Time min.	Actual Time sec.	Local Speed m.p.h.	Coal fired †	Average speed m.p.h.†	Cut-off (per cent) ‡		
0·0	Paddington		0	0	—			77	50	45
4·3	Acton		07	00	—	16	36·8	45		
9·1	Southall	11	11	50	61	21	59·6	45	40	
13·2	West Drayton		15	45	65	16	62·6	35		
18·5	Slough	20	20	30	70	20	67·0	35		
24·2	Maidenhead	25½	25	40	65	24	66·2	35		
31·0	Twyford	31½	31	55	66	27	65·3	35		
36·0	Reading*	37	36	30	45	15	65·5	35	50	
37·8	Southcote Jc.		38	50	45	4	46·3	50	40	37
53·1	Newbury	56	54	20	59	80	59·3	40		
58·5	Kintbury		60	00	57	26	57·2	43		
61·5	Hungerford		63	10	56	25	56·8	48		
66·4	Bedwyn	69½	68	30	54	24	55·1	48	50	
70·1	Savernake		73	00	45	22	49·4	50	40	35
81·1	Patney		82	55	72	49	66·6	35		
86·9	Lavington		87	00	90	18	85·1	35		
95·6	Westbury*	97½	94	00	35	30	74·5	50	40	35
01·3	Frome*		101	00	35	32	48·8	50	40	35
08·5	Brewham (M.P.122¾)	113	111	00	35	48	42·0	50	25	
15·3	Castle Cary*	120	117	00	60	12	68·0	40		
27·9	Long Sutton		127	12	79	56	74·0	40		
31·0	Curry Rivell Jc.		129	30	84	14	80·9	40		
34·9	Athelney		132	30	72	17	78·0	40		
37·9	Cogload Jc.	143	135	00	72	15	72·0	33		
42·9	Taunton	148	139	30	61	24	66·7	33	35	40
50·0	Wellington		147	30	51	33	53·3	45	50	
53·8	Whiteball Box		153	00	40	23	41·5	50	25	
58·8	Tiverton Jc.		157	15	77	17	70·6	25		
61·1	Cullompton		159	00	80	6	78·9	25		
70·2	Stoke Canon		166	20	77	28	74·5	25		
73·7	Exeter (St D.)*	179	170	00	30	10	57·3	35	30	27
82·2	Starcross		179	00	65	25	56·6	22		
93·9	Newton Abbot*	203	192	00	30	37	54·0	50	60	70
97·7	Dainton Box	209½	198	00	20	30	38·0	70	22	
02·5	Totnes	215½	203	00	60	5	57·6	50	40	60
05·3	Tigley Box		207	00	25	22	42·0	60		
07·1	Rattery Box	223	210	00	31	12	36·0	60	55	
09·4	Brent	225	213	00	50	16	46·0	50		
11·6	Wrangaton		215	30	54	—	52·9	50	22	
19·0	Hererdon Box	237	223	30	63	—	55·5	22		
21·7	Plympton		226	00	75	—	64·8	22	35	50
24·2	Lipson Jc.	245	229	00	—	—	50·9	55		
25·7	Plymouth (North Rd)	247	232	00	—	—	30·0			

* Speed restriction   † from previous timing point. Coal counted in shovelfuls,
‡ at and after the timing point   total 899.

INDEX

GENERAL

Accessibility of mechanism, 55, 136, 142
Accidents, 26; Long Ashton, 42; Weedon, 42
Air currents at front end, 178
Air pump, 105; -valves, 19
American practice, 91
Ash-disposal, 138
Ash-pan, 89; hopper-type, 113, 138
Atchison Topeka and Santa Fé 2/4–6–0, 79, 96A
Atmospheric railways, 26
Axleboxes, 30; knock, 87; tightly-fitting, 42
Axles, overloaded, 32, 33, 46

Barge, Thames, 30
Beyer, Peacock & Co., 48
Bihta derailment, 37
Bluebell Railway, 72
Bogie, 36, 46; of Dean singles, 47; withdrawn to get at valves, 46, 79
Boiler, -changes, 48; -cradle, 24, 84, 104; -pressure, 39, 111; -supports, 41
Brakes, 41; one-wheel, 37; sledge, 37, 57; steam, 69, 176
Brecon & Merthyr Rly, 68
Bridges, 24
Bristol & Exeter Rly, 41
Bristolian, 70, 107

Bunk, 76
Bunker, 44
Burning of enginemen, 20

Cabs, 39, 42, 44; longroof, 64, 80A; with no outside foot-hold, 112
Centenary, Baltimore & Ohio, 77; Railway (1925), 76
Char-disposal, 138
Cheltenham Flyer (previously Tea-car train), 70, 106, 107
Chief mechanical engineers, 20
Chimney, dominating, 114, 142; double, 112, 113, 140, 142, 143
Coal, consumption, 132; double handling, 7, 137, 155
Combustion-chamber, 66
Compound engines, French, 18, 88, 89, 140
Compound expansion, 81
Condensing engines, 38, 45
Coupling-rods, 35
Cow-catcher, 79
Cramlington Colliery Co., 68
Crank-axles, 78
Cut-off, 85, 96, 105, 149
Cylinder-casting, 32

Dean singles, 33
Defective locomotives, 29
Derailment, Bihta, 37; Box Tunnel 46